BAKE

PAUL HOLLYWOOD

BAKE

My best ever recipes for the classics

Photography by Haarala Hamilton

BLOOMSBURY PUBLISHING

NEW YORK • LONDON • OXFORD • NEW DELHI • SYDNEY

CONTENTS

A passion for baking

Baking is all about sharing. Even after more than three decades in many different professional roles, nothing beats making something for someone else and seeing their eyes light up when they taste it. It brings me pure joy and is a real privilege. It's not been an easy task choosing my favorite classic recipes for this book, and everyone will have their own view of what those classic bakes should be, but these are my classics. These are the recipes I enjoy, that I have refined and perfected over the years. I have judged, tested and tasted literally thousands of cakes, cookies, pastries and desserts, and have probably baked as many myself! Each time I taste or bake something, I learn something new and am inspired to improve and develop my recipes further. This collection brings together all my ultimate versions of the recipes that are special to me, adjusted, updated and honed to be the very best they can. I want to share these recipes with you so you can enjoy making them as much as I do.

When you've baked something yourself – when it comes out of your oven, filling your kitchen with the smell of banana bread, a sponge cake or a great loaf – you'll appreciate it so much more. Even better, it means you can share that experience with others: your family, friends, colleagues or neighbors. I think, ultimately, we're all very nostalgic, and baking taps right into that.

We love the memory of something our grandmothers used to bake for us. You bite into it, and it takes you straight back to eating it when you were five or six years old. I think people really yearn for these kinds of memories, and you usually don't have to dig all that far into most people's history to find a family recipe. If you don't already have that connection in your life with someone who bakes a lot, then the recipes in this book are an opportunity for you to be that person for someone else, to pass know-how on to those in your life so we don't lose these skills and associations. A tray of cookies still warm from the oven or a slice of freshly baked cake means more than you realize at the time and will create treasured lasting memories.

I honestly feel that baking is in our DNA. From local fairs and bake sales to school fundraisers, everyone wants to share their homemade creations and be known for making the best lemon cake, the gooiest chocolate brownie, the crumbliest shortbread or the flakiest pastry. It's like there are mini *Bake Offs* happening all over the place, and there always have been. I think we often overlook how good at baking we are in the UK but it's something we should be proud of. I love to be surprised and inspired by what people produce, and I enjoy seeing the passion for baking in people's faces. It's that baking passion that keeps them going, and I can completely relate because I share it too.

Baking around the world

It's fascinating to me how baking has evolved and developed over time, and from country to country. As people have moved around the globe, we've picked up techniques, styles and ingredients and we've experimented with them and adapted them. We've made use of regional recipes and local ingredients, from the dates and honey of the Middle East to the sugar and sweet fruits of the West Indies, and we've incorporated them into our own baking. A lot depends on the climate where you live, too. For example, it will determine what grain thrives best in the area and that grain will dominate in local baking. In Eastern and Northern Europe, you'll find breads made with rye flour which can better tolerate cold conditions; whereas in milder climates, lighter types of flour like wheat are more commonly produced. I really enjoy working with ingredients from different parts of the world, learning what they bring to baking and how to get the most from their unique qualities.

I've been incredibly lucky during my professional and personal life to have worked in and traveled to some amazing locations and to have tried so much incredible food. These experiences have had a huge influence on the kinds of recipes I bake today. From my time living in Cyprus to trips across the United States, and learning from the best in Italy, France, Spain and elsewhere, I have taken inspiration from all around me. But, of course, at my heart I'm a northern lad. And I will always be drawn back to my roots in the north-west of England. That's where I grew up and that's where I first learned my trade. That's why you'll find in this collection of classics, almond and orange biscotti (page 65), New York chocolate brownie cheesecake (page 36) and beef empanadas (page 216) sitting comfortably alongside those timeless British favorites, cheese scones (page 80), pigs in blankets (page 202) and savory pies, and in a nod to my northern upbringing, barm cakes (page 116) and bin lids (page 118). If you are not familiar with bin lids, I urge you to make one so you can have the best "chip butty" of your life!

Back to bread

At the heart of almost every culture in the world you'll find some kind of bread, and you can tell a lot about the history of a society by the breads it baked. Back in the day, nomadic communities didn't have bread ovens like we do today. Instead, they'd bake over fires, almost like a broiler, producing amazing, quick flatbreads. I love how versatile flatbreads are. It's a very basic dough but tastes fantastic topped with your favorite ingredients, used as a wrap, or for dipping. From tortillas (page 149) and naans (page 140) to lesser-known flatbreads like maneesh (page 146) and lagana (page 142), I've included some of my absolute favorites for you to try.

As people started to settle in one place for longer periods of time, they began to build dedicated bread ovens. This is when the kinds of breads we are more used to today (that use raising agents) were developed. They required slow proofing and longer cooking, so were more suited to communities that weren't frequently on the move.

Of course, it's no surprise that I've included plenty of great bread recipes here, from my fail-safe sandwich loaves (pages 92, 96 and 108) and traditional sourdough (page 121) to a rich cheesy bread (page 113) and a lovely sweet orange brioche (page 132). For me, the bread thing started from a really early age.

My mother was great at making biscuits and pastries, but my father was the bread and pie man. He would always come home from work at his bakery smelling of bread. It's the same with me now – I love my pastry, scones and doughnuts, but it's bread that's my real passion. When I joined the industry, I started out working at my father's bakery and the first thing I learned was how to make a proper loaf. My father put me with the best guys who mixed and shaped the dough on the table, and who ran the ovens. They taught me so much and I'm so grateful to them. Through these recipes, I'll share my top tips with you too.

Something sweet

Anyone who knows me knows that I have a sweet tooth, and in this book I've brought together all my favorite sweet treats. Whether you want a comforting apple or pecan pie that reminds you of cozy days at home with your family (page 218 or 231), or you're looking to impress with a showstopper of a dessert, like a baked Alaska or chocolate and raspberry entremets (page 264 or 290), the beauty of baking is there's something for every occasion and every mood.

Honestly, though, I don't think there's much better in life than a cup of tea with a slice of cake or a homemade cookie. Baking trends will come and go (we've had cronuts and cruffins, and who knows what's next) but you can't beat the classics – a Victoria sandwich (page 20), carrot cake (page 30), ginger snap (page 68) or a buttered scone (page 79). One of the reasons I think baking has stayed so universally popular is that it mostly uses really basic ingredients and at its core it's simple to do. The majority of people will have the ingredients to make a Victoria sandwich in their cupboards right now. Baking is approachable, relatively cheap and most of the time needs only very standard pieces of kit.

Make it
your own

Baking can also be very personal. We all have our likes and dislikes and it's a real chance to make it your own, to put your spin on recipes and start creating your own family traditions. It's about learning and experimenting, and I'm always looking to practice new techniques or develop old ones.

Nothing about baking is tricky, so if you've not done much before then I hope these recipes will encourage you to give it a go. They're true, tried-and-tested classics you can rely on to create perfect bakes every time. As we say before the technical challenges on *The Great British Bake Off*: just read the recipe all the way through beforehand and you'll be absolutely fine. Then, once you feel comfortable with the basics, feel free to add your own twist to the recipes. If you enjoy baking and eating something you've made, you'll quickly find that other people will join you – and maybe add their take on things too. It's a really exciting time for baking, with access to so many amazing ingredients and world influences.

Next time you visit someone's house, bake a cake or a loaf of bread and take it with you instead of a bottle of wine or some chocolates. There's nothing like making something yourself. The processes involved, the fact you can share the experience with your kids and family; it creates those all-important precious, lasting memories.

A note on measurements:

- Flour, sugar and cocoa cup measures are spooned and leveled.
- Brown sugar measurements are firmly packed.
- Other non-liquid cup measurements are loosely packed.
- Measurements in cups and in metric weight have both been given but please use only one set of measurements.

0

1

2

Cakes

In the UK, we are very good at eating cake! I think all baking is nostalgic, but cake is probably the bake that instantly conjures up the most memories. From birthday cakes to bake sales, cakes tend to take you right back to being a kid.

When I was working in hotels, a good cake meant something that would go well with a cup of tea. From my rich and sticky ginger loaf to a traditional cherry cake, chocolate orange banana bread and white chocolate blondies (pages 24, 26, 18 and 52 respectively), the cakes in this chapter all go beautifully with a "brew". I think one of the best meals of the day is a proper afternoon tea, and I'll often pull out all the stops when I have people visiting. Sandwiches, scones with some preserves and cream, and little slices of cake. Perfect.

Baking a cake is, in many ways, a lot simpler than other kinds of baking. With bread, you're working with the dough, kneading and shaping it, and it can take a few goes to really know what you're looking for. With cakes, as long as you measure everything out correctly and mix it together properly, you can't go far wrong. Baking cakes is pure science – if possible, use a digital weighing scale for accuracy and I have given the metric weights to help with this. If you have a good set of scales and follow the instructions, you can bake any cake you wish.

Most cakes are made with the same core ingredients – flour, eggs, butter and sugar – and then it comes down to the flavors you want to add. That could be bananas, ginger, raisins, cherries, chocolate or whatever you fancy. When you're adding flavors, just make sure they pack a punch. That goes for any ganache or filling too – you really want to be able to taste it as you bite through the layers.

This chapter is a real winner with some truly classic recipes, many of which have been part of British baking history for a long time, like my favorite cake of all, the lemon drizzle on page 32. For something all-out decadent, the chocolate fudge cake on page 34 will hit the spot, or if you're after a more elegant bake, the chocolate hazelnut torte on page 29 is sure to impress. Although it's not baked, I've also included one of my absolute favorites: a berry fruits cheesecake on page 43. The combination of textures from the crunchy base, creamy filling and fresh fruit topping is amazing. Pure heaven.

Chocolate Orange Banana Bread

8–10 slices

4 ripe bananas

1¼ cups (250g) superfine sugar

1 stick plus 1 tbsp (125g) **unsalted butter**, softened, plus extra to grease the pan

Finely grated zest of 1 orange

2 large eggs

2 cups (250g) all-purpose flour

2 tsp baking powder

½ cup (75g) bittersweet chocolate chips

Tangy orange zest and chunks of bittersweet chocolate folded into the mix give everyone's favorite banana bread an upgrade. It has a delicious richness and wonderful intensity of flavor, yet it's not overly sweet.

Heat your oven to 350°F. Grease and line a 2-pound (1kg) loaf pan with parchment paper.

Roughly chop 3 bananas and put them in a large bowl with the sugar, butter and orange zest. Whisk using an electric hand whisk until smoothly combined. Add the eggs, one at a time, beating well after each addition.

Mix the flour and baking powder together, then sift over the banana mixture and gently fold in until evenly combined. Fold in the chocolate chips.

Spoon the mixture into the prepared loaf pan and gently smooth the surface to level it. Cut the remaining banana in half lengthwise and gently press, cut side up, onto the surface of the mixture.

Bake for 50–60 minutes until risen and golden brown. To check the banana bread is cooked, insert a skewer into the center; it should come out clean. Remove from the pan and put on a wire rack to cool.

Victoria Sandwich

8–10 slices

If you're new to baking, this should be your very first cake. If you get it right, everything else will be easy. You can make a Victoria sandwich using the all-in-one method, where you mix everything together in a bowl at the same time, but I encourage you to cream the fats and sugar together before adding the eggs, flour and raising agent, as you'll learn a lot about baking this way. Baking is a science. That's why, if possible, I prefer to weigh the eggs first and then adjust the quantities of the other ingredients to get the perfect balance. I like to use half margarine for a lighter texture and half butter for a rich flavor. Traditionally, it's filled with just preserves, but if you're feeling indulgent, feel free to add whipped cream or buttercream.

———

4 large eggs (in their shells)

1¼ cups (about 240g) superfine sugar

1¾ cups plus 3 tbsp (about 240g) all-purpose flour

3 tsp baking powder

1 stick (about 120g) unsalted butter, softened, plus extra to grease the pans

1 stick (about 120g) margarine, softened

To finish

½ cup (125g) raspberry preserves (good-quality)

A little superfine sugar, to sprinkle

Heat your oven to 350°F. Grease two 8-inch (20cm) cake pans and line the bases with parchment paper. Weigh the eggs first (in their shells), then weigh the same quantity of sugar and flour. For the butter and the margarine, you need half the weight of the eggs.

In a large bowl, cream the butter, margarine and sugar together using an electric whisk until pale in color and light and fluffy (**1**). Scrape down the sides of the bowl and beat again.

Beat the eggs together in a pitcher, then gradually add to the mixture, beating well after each addition (**2**). Scrape down the sides of the bowl and mix again. Sift the flour and baking powder over the surface of the mixture and gently fold in, using a large metal spoon (**3**).

Divide the mixture between the prepared cake pans. To ensure the cakes are exactly the same size you can weigh the cake mixture into each pan. Gently smooth the surface with the back of the spoon to level it (**4**).

Bake in the center of the oven for 25 minutes until risen, golden brown and the cakes spring back in the center when lightly touched with a fingertip. They should be slightly shrunken away from the edges of the pan. Leave the cakes in the pans for 5 minutes, then remove to a wire rack. Leave to cool completely.

When cold, sandwich the cakes together with the raspberry preserves and sprinkle the top with a little superfine sugar.

Steps illustrated overleaf

Sticky Ginger Loaf

8–10 slices

I love ginger – I even have it in my gin and tonic! This gorgeous sticky ginger loaf includes crystallized ginger as well as ground ginger, which lends sweetness, and it is topped with a lemon-flavored glacé icing. It's lovely for afternoon tea, but you can enjoy it any time of day – just as it is or spread with a little butter.

1⅔ cups (200g) all-purpose flour

2¾ tsp baking powder

1 tbsp ground ginger

1 tsp ground cinnamon

¼ tsp ground cloves

7 tbsp (100g) unsalted butter, plus extra to grease the pan

7 tbsp (125g) Lyle's golden syrup

7 tbsp (125g) molasses

½ cup (100g) dark brown sugar

1 large egg

⅔ cup (150g) whole milk

½ cup (90g) finely chopped crystallized ginger

To finish

¾ cup (75g) confectioners' sugar, sifted

2 tbsp lemon juice

2–3 pieces crystallized ginger, chopped

Heat your oven to 350°F. Grease and line a 2-pound (1kg) loaf pan with parchment paper.

In a large bowl, mix the flour, baking powder and ground spices together and then make a well in the middle.

In a small saucepan over a medium heat, heat the butter, golden syrup, molasses and brown sugar together until the butter is melted. Pour into the flour mixture and stir until evenly combined.

In another bowl, beat the egg with the milk then gradually stir this into the mixture until it is all incorporated. Fold through the chopped crystallized ginger.

Pour the mixture into the prepared loaf pan and bake for 40–45 minutes until risen and golden. To check the cake is cooked, insert a skewer into the center; it should come out clean.

Leave the cake to cool in the pan for 10 minutes, then remove, transfer to a wire rack and leave to cool completely.

For the glacé icing, mix the confectioners' sugar with the lemon juice to form a paste. Thin the icing with a splash of water if necessary – it should be thin enough to run off the spoon. Drizzle the icing over the cooled cake and sprinkle with the chopped crystallized ginger to finish.

Cherry Cake

6–8 slices

Like the Victoria sandwich, I think cherry cake is one of those truly classic cakes that needs to be in every baker's repertoire. This version includes almond flour, which helps it stay moist so it will keep for longer. Candied cherries give it a burst of sweetness and color.

———

1⅓ cups (165g) all-purpose flour

2 tsp baking powder

⅔ cup (110g) superfine sugar

1 stick (110g) margarine or **butter**, softened, plus extra to grease the pan

2 large eggs

⅔ cup (65g) almond flour

1 tbsp whole milk

1 cup (165g) candied cherries, halved

16 whole skinned almonds

Heat your oven to 325°F. Grease and line a 6-inch (15cm) springform pan with parchment paper.

Put all the ingredients except the cherries and almonds into a stand mixer fitted with the paddle attachment. Start mixing on a low speed until the ingredients are combined. Increase the speed and mix for 1 minute until the mixture is smooth and pale.

Fold three-quarters of the candied cherries into the mixture. Spoon into the lined springform pan and gently smooth the top to level it.

Sprinkle over the remaining candied cherries and poke them into the surface of the cake. Arrange the whole almonds over the surface and gently press these in too. Bake for 1 hour until the cake is risen, lightly golden and springs back when gently pressed in the center.

Leave the cake to cool in the pan for 10 minutes then turn out onto a wire rack and leave to cool completely.

Chocolate Hazelnut Torte

10 slices

This is a deceptively easy cake, made using ingredients you might already have in your kitchen cupboards. There are a few more stages involved, such as making a sugar syrup and melting the chocolate, but it isn't difficult and the end result looks really impressive.

———

1 cup plus 1 tbsp (210g) superfine sugar

½ cup plus 1 tsp (130g) water

10 oz (300g) bittersweet chocolate, broken into small pieces

1 stick plus 2 tbsp (150g) unsalted butter, cut into pieces, plus extra to grease the pan

4 large eggs

3 tbsp all-purpose flour

½ cup (50g) hazelnuts, skinned, toasted and roughly chopped

Amaretto cream

1 cup (250g) heavy cream

3 tbsp Amaretto liqueur

2 tbsp confectioners' sugar, sifted

To finish

Unsweetened cocoa powder

Heat your oven to 375°F. Grease a 9-inch (21cm) springform pan and line the base with parchment paper.

In a saucepan, heat ⅔ cup (130g) of the sugar with the water until dissolved to form a sugar syrup.

Melt the chocolate and butter together in a heatproof bowl over a saucepan of simmering water, making sure the base of the bowl is not touching the water.

Using a stand mixer fitted with the whisk attachment, beat the eggs and remaining ⅓ cup plus 1 tablespoon (80g) sugar until tripled in volume. Add the sugar syrup and melted chocolate mixture and whisk to combine.

Sift the flour over the mixture and gently fold in, along with the chopped nuts. Spoon the mixture into the prepared pan and bake for 40–45 minutes until firm. Leave to cool completely before removing from the pan.

For the Amaretto cream, whip the cream in a bowl until it forms soft peaks, then fold in the liqueur and confectioners' sugar.

Dust the surface of the cake with cocoa powder and serve each slice with a good dollop of the Amaretto cream on the side.

Carrot Cake

8 slices

My gently spiced carrot cake uses a mixture of whole wheat and all-purpose flours for extra depth. Grated carrots and oil keep it deliciously moist, and chopped walnuts add crunch and flavor. The smooth cream cheese frosting is the perfect complement, while walnut halves and toasted coconut chips add a contrasting finish. Here I've piped the frosting but you can simply spread it on if you prefer.

1¼ cups (150g) all-purpose flour

¾ cup plus 1 tbsp (100g) whole wheat pastry flour

2 tsp baking powder

½ tsp fine salt

1½ tsp ground cinnamon

A pinch of ground cloves

½ tsp ground nutmeg

¾ cup plus 1 tbsp (180g) vegetable oil, plus extra to oil the pans

½ cup (100g) superfine sugar

½ cup (100g) light brown sugar

3 large eggs

1 tsp vanilla extract

Finely grated zest and juice of 1 orange

2 cups (200g) grated carrots

1 cup (100g) walnuts, chopped

½ cup (25g) coconut chips

Cream cheese frosting

5 tbsp (75g) butter, at room temperature

½ cup (50g) confectioners' sugar

1¼ cups/10 oz (300g) cream cheese, at room temperature

To finish

Walnut halves

Toasted coconut chips

Heat your oven to 350°F. Grease two 8-inch (20cm) cake pans and line the bases with parchment paper.

In a bowl, mix the flours, baking powder, salt and ground spices together and make a well in the middle.

In a separate bowl, whisk the oil, sugars, eggs, vanilla extract and the orange zest and juice together until well combined.

Pour the whisked mixture into the flour mix and stir until you have a smooth batter. Stir in the grated carrots, chopped walnuts and coconut chips.

Divide the mixture between the prepared pans and smooth the surface to level. Bake for 25–30 minutes until the cake is risen and springy to the touch.

In the meantime, make the cream cheese frosting. In a bowl, using a hand-held electric whisk, beat the butter until soft, then add the confectioners' sugar and beat well until creamy. Finally add the cream cheese and beat until just combined. Cover and chill until ready to use.

Once cooked, leave the cakes to cool in the pans for 15 minutes then turn out onto a wire rack and leave to cool completely.

To assemble, put the cream cheese frosting into a pastry bag fitted with a ½-inch (1cm) plain tip. Pipe half the icing over one of the cooled cakes and sandwich together with the other cake. Pipe the remaining frosting decoratively on top of the cake and finish with walnut halves and toasted coconut chips.

Lemon Drizzle Cake

8–10 slices

This is my favorite cake of all time. I love it when we have to judge this round on *The Great British Bake Off*! The perfect lemon drizzle has a light and airy sponge and a sharp, zesty crunchy topping. My version has quite an intense lemony flavor, but other than that it's a total classic and I don't think you should mess with those classics. The only thing to remember is to pour over the drizzle while the cake is still warm.

1 stick plus 4 tbsp (175g) butter, softened, plus extra to grease the pan

¾ cup plus 2 tbsp (175g) superfine sugar

Finely grated zest of 2 lemons

3 large eggs

1⅓ cups (175g) all-purpose flour

2½ tsp baking powder

A pinch of fine salt

About 2 tbsp whole milk

Drizzle topping

Juice of 1 lemon

2 tbsp granulated sugar

Heat your oven to 350°F. Grease and line a 2-pound (1kg) loaf pan with parchment paper.

In a large bowl, beat the butter, sugar and lemon zest together, using a hand-held electric whisk, until the mixture is very light and fluffy.

Add the eggs one at a time, beating well after each addition. Add the flour, baking powder and salt and mix until smoothly combined. Add just enough milk to achieve a dropping consistency.

Spoon the mixture into the prepared loaf pan and gently smooth the surface to level it. Bake for 45–50 minutes or until a skewer inserted into the center comes out clean.

Once you've removed the cake from the oven, make the drizzle topping: mix the lemon juice and sugar together in a small pitcher. While the cake is still warm, use a toothpick to prick holes all over the top of the cake then trickle over the lemon drizzle. Leave to cool completely in the pan before removing.

Chocolate Fudge Cake

10 slices

If you love chocolate cake, then you have to try this one. It is a real crowd-pleaser: not particularly rich but sweet, gooey and delicious. Using margarine rather than butter keeps it light, and the brown sugar adds color and a hint of caramel. It makes a fantastic birthday cake too – just stick a candle in the middle and both kids and adults will want an extra slice once they've tried it.

1 stick plus 4 tbsp (175g) margarine, softened, plus extra to grease the pans

1 cup plus 2 tbsp (225g) light brown sugar

1 cup (200g) superfine sugar

3 large eggs

1 tsp vanilla extract

2 cups (250g) all-purpose flour

1¼ cups (125g) unsweetened cocoa powder

1½ tsp baking powder

½ tsp fine salt

1½ cups (375g) sour cream

Chocolate frosting

6 oz (150g) bittersweet chocolate, broken into small pieces

1 cup (100g) unsweetened cocoa powder

7 tbsp (100g) boiling water

2 sticks (225g) unsalted butter, softened

6 tbsp confectioners' sugar

Heat your oven to 350°F. Grease three 8-inch (20cm) cake pans and line the bases with parchment paper.

Using a stand mixer fitted with the whisk attachment, beat the margarine and sugars together until the mixture is pale and fluffy; this will take around 5 minutes. Scrape down the sides of the bowl with a spatula and whisk again.

In a separate bowl, beat the eggs with the vanilla extract. With the mixer still running on a low-medium speed, slowly pour the beaten eggs into the mixture.

Sift the flour with the cocoa powder, baking powder and salt. Add a large spoonful to the whisked mixture and stir in, then mix in a large spoonful of the sour cream. Repeat until all the flour and sour cream are incorporated. Beat until you have a smooth batter.

Divide the batter equally between the prepared pans. Bake for 20–25 minutes until the cakes are risen and slightly shrunk away from the sides of the pan. Leave to cool in the pans before transferring to a wire rack to cool completely.

To make the chocolate frosting, melt the chocolate in a heatproof bowl set over a saucepan of simmering water, making sure the base of the bowl is not in contact with the water. Stir until smooth and set aside to cool. In another bowl, mix the cocoa powder with the boiling water to make a thick paste.

In a large bowl, beat the butter until soft and fluffy then add the confectioners' sugar and whisk until pale and fluffy. Add the melted chocolate and cocoa paste and beat until the frosting is smooth.

To assemble the cake, put one cake layer on your serving plate and spread with a quarter of the frosting. Put a second cake layer on top and spread with another quarter of the frosting. Position the final cake layer on top and cover the top and sides with the remaining frosting. Leave the frosting to set before cutting the cake.

New York Chocolate Brownie Cheesecake

8–10 slices

I came across a cheesecake like this when I was over at Junior's restaurant in New York, which is famous for its amazing cheesecakes. It's a vanilla mixture swirled through a chocolate brownie mix and baked on a sponge base – it's incredible. The secret to achieving a velvety texture is to mix the filling very slowly so that you don't incorporate any air and to then bake it in a water bath so it cooks gently and evenly.

———

Base

⅓ cup plus 1 tbsp (50g) all-purpose flour

1 tsp baking powder

A pinch of fine salt

2 large eggs, separated

¼ cup (50g) superfine sugar

Finely grated zest of ½ lemon

2 tbsp (30g) butter, melted, plus extra to grease the pan

¼ tsp cream of tartar

Chocolate brownie mix

14 oz (400g) bittersweet chocolate

2 sticks (225g) unsalted butter

3 large eggs

1 cup plus 2 tbsp (225g) superfine sugar

⅔ cup (75g) all-purpose flour

1 tsp baking powder

½ tsp fine salt

Vanilla filling mix

1⅔ cups/14 oz (400g) cream cheese

1 tbsp cornstarch

¼ cup (50g) superfine sugar

2 large eggs

1½ tsp vanilla extract

½ cup (120g) heavy cream

Heat your oven to 345°F. Grease a 9-inch (23cm) springform pan and line the base with parchment paper.

To prepare the base, sift the flour, baking powder and salt into a bowl and set aside. In a large bowl, beat the egg yolks with a hand-held electric whisk for 2 minutes. Add 2 tablespoons of the sugar and whisk until the mixture is thick and reaches the ribbon stage (i.e. when the whisk is lifted up the trail of mix that falls from it will form a ribbon in the surface); this will take around 5 minutes (**1**). Add the flour mix and carefully fold in, followed by the lemon zest and melted butter.

In a clean large bowl, whisk the egg whites together with the cream of tartar until stiff peaks form. Gradually add the remaining sugar, beating well after each addition, until it is all incorporated and you have a meringue that holds glossy peaks. Fold a large spoonful of the meringue into the egg yolk mix, then carefully fold in the rest.

Tip the mixture into the prepared springform pan (**2**) and gently level the surface. Bake for 12–14 minutes until the sponge springs back when touched gently (**3**); it should be pale in color. Stand the pan on a wire rack and leave to cool.

Once the sponge is cooled, wrap a sheet of foil around the springform pan (under the base and around the side) to seal it (and prevent water from entering during cooking, as the cheesecake is baked in a water bath).

For the chocolate brownie mixture, melt the chocolate and butter in a heatproof bowl over a saucepan of simmering water, making sure the base of the bowl is not touching the water (**4**). Remove from the heat and let cool, then beat in the eggs, one at a time. Stir in the sugar, then fold through the flour, baking powder and salt.

Continued overleaf

Pour the chocolate brownie mix over the sponge base and stand the foil-wrapped springform pan in a deep roasting pan.

To prepare the vanilla filling mix, in a large bowl, very slowly beat scant 1 cup/ 7 oz (200g) of the cream cheese with the cornstarch and 2 tablespoons of the sugar, using a hand-held electric whisk, until smooth. Whisk in the remaining cream cheese and sugar, again on a slow speed. You'll need to keep scraping the sides of the bowl. Don't be tempted to rush this stage.

Now beat in the eggs, one at a time, on a medium speed. Add the vanilla extract and heavy cream and beat until just combined.

Pour the vanilla mix into the cake pan and carefully swirl it through the brownie mixture, using a skewer (**5**).

Pour enough cold water into the roasting pan to come about 1 inch (2½cm) up the side of the springform pan (**6**). Bake for 1 hour or until the edges of the cheesecake are lightly golden and the center of the cheesecake has a slight wobble.

Lift the springform pan onto a wire rack and leave the cheesecake to cool completely. Once cold, cover the pan with plastic wrap and put in the fridge overnight or for at least 4 hours.

To serve, carefully release the cheesecake from the pan and cut into slices, using a heated knife. Eat just as is, or with a little pouring cream.

Steps continued overleaf

3

4

5

6

Berry Fruits Cheesecake

10 slices

Although this isn't a baked cheesecake, it's such a classic for me that I had to include it. My mum used to make it when I was a kid and it was a massive favorite of mine. It still is now. I love the tartness of the fruit topping, the sweetness of the creamy vanilla and berry interior, and the crumbly cracker crumb base. It's got everything.

_____

Base

7 oz (approx 12 sheets/200g) graham crackers

1 stick plus 2 tbsp (150g) unsalted butter, melted, plus extra to grease the pan

Berry filling

1¾ tsp unflavored gelatin powder

1 cup (100g) frozen berry fruits, thawed

1¼ cups/10 oz (300g) cream cheese

2 tbsp superfine sugar

¾ cup (175g) heavy cream

¼ cup (60g) just-boiled water

Vanilla filling

1¾ tsp unflavored gelatin powder

1¼ cups/10 oz (300g) cream cheese

2 tbsp superfine sugar

1 tsp vanilla extract

¾ cup (175g) heavy cream

¼ cup (60g) just-boiled water

Topping

1 tsp unflavored gelatin powder

⅔ cup (150g) red berry juice

1½ cups (150g) mixed berry fruits (cherries, blueberries, blackberries, raspberries)

Lightly grease a 9-inch (23cm) springform pan with butter and line the base and sides with parchment paper.

For the base, put the graham crackers into a strong freezer bag and bash with a rolling pin to a crumb-like texture. Transfer to a bowl, pour on the melted butter and stir until the crumbs are fully coated. Tip the crumb mixture into the prepared springform pan, spread it evenly and press down firmly onto the base, using the back of a spoon. Chill until set firm.

To make the berry filling, put 2 tablespoons of cold water into a medium-sized heatproof bowl, sprinkle over the gelatin and set aside to hydrate. Meanwhile, using a blender or food processor, blitz the thawed berries to a purée.

In a large bowl, beat the cream cheese with the sugar until smooth. Add the puréed fruit and stir to combine. In another bowl, whip the cream to soft peaks and then fold into the fruit and cream cheese mix.

Pour the ¼ cup (60g) just-boiled water onto the gelatin and stir until fully dissolved, then fold into the berry filling until well combined. Pour onto the cracker crumb base, smooth the surface to level and put in the fridge to set for an hour.

To make the vanilla filling, put 2 tablespoons of cold water into a medium-sized heatproof bowl, sprinkle over the gelatin and set aside to hydrate. Meanwhile, in a large bowl, mix the cream cheese with the sugar and vanilla extract until smooth. Whip the cream to soft peaks and fold into the cream cheese mix.

Continued overleaf

Pour the ¼ cup (60g) just-boiled water onto the gelatin and stir until fully dissolved, then fold into the cream cheese mixture until well combined. Pour the mixture onto the set berry filling and smooth the surface to level. Return to the fridge for another hour to set the vanilla layer.

For the topping, put 2 tablespoons of cold water into a medium-sized heatproof bowl. Sprinkle over the gelatin and set aside to hydrate. Heat the berry juice in a small saucepan; do not let it boil. Pour ¼ cup of the the berry juice over the gelatin and stir until fully dissolved, then add this gelatin mixture to the remaining juice and stir until well combined. Transfer the juice mixture to a heatproof pitcher and leave to cool, until slightly thickened but still pourable.

Arrange the berries on top of the set cheesecake then carefully pour the thickened berry juice over them and the surface of the cheesecake. Put in the fridge to set.

To serve, carefully release the cheesecake from the pan and transfer to a serving plate. Use a warmed knife to cut into neat slices.

Blueberry Muffins

Makes 12

An all-American hero of a bake, these blueberry muffins are made with butter, which gives them extra flavor and richness and a more cake-like texture. Perfect for any time of day, I particularly like to enjoy mine with a cup of coffee in the morning.

4¼ cups (550g) all-purpose flour

2 tbsp plus ½ tsp baking powder

1 cup plus 2 tbsp (230g) superfine sugar

1 tsp fine salt

3 sticks (350g) cold unsalted butter, diced

2 large eggs

¾ cup plus 1 tbsp (200g) whole milk

1 tsp vanilla extract

1¾ cups (230g) blueberries

———

Heat your oven to 400°F. Line a 12-cup muffin pan with paper muffin liners.

In a large bowl, mix the flour, baking powder, sugar and salt together. Using your fingers, rub in the butter until the mixture resembles fine breadcrumbs. Make a well in the center.

In another bowl, beat the eggs with the milk and vanilla extract. Pour into the flour mix and stir until combined. Fold in the blueberries.

Spoon the mixture into the paper muffin liners, so that it comes fairly near the top of each liner. Bake for 20 minutes or until the muffins are risen and golden, and a skewer inserted into the center of one comes out clean.

Leave to cool in the pan for a few minutes then transfer the muffins to a wire rack to finish cooling.

Chocolate Brownies

Makes 12–15

Even if I say it myself, these are the best brownies you'll ever taste. Chunks of milk and bittersweet chocolate are folded through the mix for extra richness, while the cacao nibs scattered on top provide nuttiness and a little crunch. Perfect with a cup of tea, they're equally delicious still slightly warm from the oven with a scoop of ice cream.

———

8 oz (225g) semisweet chocolate (35–45% cocoa solids), broken into small pieces

2 sticks (225g) unsalted butter, in pieces

3 large eggs

1 cup plus 2 tbsp (225g) superfine sugar

⅔ cup (75g) all-purpose flour

1 tsp baking powder

½ tsp fine salt

½ cup (100g) bittersweet chocolate chips

½ cup (100g) milk chocolate chips

1 tsp vanilla extract

1 tbsp cacao nibs

Heat your oven to 350°F. Line a 9 x 13 inches (23 x 33cm) rectangular pan with parchment paper.

Melt the chocolate with the butter in a heatproof bowl set over a saucepan of simmering water, making sure the base of the bowl is not touching the water. Stir until smooth and set aside to cool.

In a large bowl, beat the eggs and sugar together, using a hand-held electric whisk, until pale and thickened. Add the melted chocolate and butter mix and fold in until thoroughly combined. Fold in the flour, baking powder, salt, chocolate chips and vanilla extract.

Pour the mixture into the prepared pan and sprinkle over the cacao nibs. Bake for 20–30 minutes until the top is cracked and crusty. To check that it is ready, insert a skewer into the center; as you remove it a little mixture should still stick to the skewer.

Leave the brownie to cool completely in the pan then cut into individual pieces. Store in an airtight container.

Blondies

Makes 12

Like brownies, blondies are an incredibly useful go-to recipe, giving a huge amount of satisfaction for something you can make in around an hour. These blondies include one of my favorite flavor combinations: white chocolate and raspberry, while the pistachio nuts provide great texture. Perfect for afternoon tea or, realistically, morning coffee...

———

2 sticks plus 1 tbsp (250g) unsalted butter, plus extra to grease the pan

3 large eggs

1¼ cups (250g) superfine sugar

1⅓ cups (175g) all-purpose flour

2 tbsp (20g) white chocolate chips

¾ cup (100g) raw pistachio nuts, chopped

2 tbsp freeze-dried raspberries

To finish

4 oz (100g) white chocolate, in pieces

Heaping ⅓ cup (50g) raw pistachio nuts, chopped

2 tsp freeze-dried raspberries

Heat your oven to 350°F. Grease a 7 x 11 inches (18 x 28cm) rectangular pan and line the base and sides with parchment paper.

Melt the butter in a saucepan over a low heat or in a microwave oven on low. Set aside to cool.

Using a hand-held electric whisk, beat the eggs and sugar together until pale, mousse-like and doubled in size. When the whisk is lifted, the trail of mix that falls should leave a ribbon on the surface of the mixture.

With the whisk on a low-medium speed, add the melted butter a little at a time, making sure each addition is fully incorporated before adding the next.

Sift the flour over the surface of the mixture and fold in gently until smoothly combined. Add the chocolate chips, pistachios and dried raspberries, and fold in until evenly distributed.

Pour the mixture into the pan, and bake for 35–40 minutes or until just cooked through. When a skewer is inserted into the center, a little mixture should still stick to it as you remove it. Leave to cool in the pan.

When ready to finish, melt the white chocolate in a heatproof bowl set over a pan of simmering water, making sure the base of the bowl is not in contact with the water. Stir until smooth and set aside to cool.

Drizzle the melted chocolate over the surface of the blondie and scatter over the chopped pistachios and freeze-dried raspberries. Leave until the chocolate is set then cut into squares. Store in an airtight container.

1

2

3

Cookies and Scones

So, what is the difference between a snap cookie and a regular cookie? It all depends on the amount of sugar and butter used in the recipe: the more sugar, the more it will snap; the more butter, the softer it will be and you'll even be able to fold or bend it without it immediately breaking. To me, a cookie that folds is a regular cookie. A cookie also tends to be slightly bigger and thicker. Snap cookies (known as biscuits in Britain) on the other hand are all about the perfect snap. They need to make a satisfying audible snap, and you should see the crumbs fly across the table. To achieve a good snap, but without the cookie being overly sweet, it's about getting that balance between sweetness and texture – between sugar and butter.

For Americans, a cookie is really anything you could conceivably dunk in a cup of tea. Although, actually, that would be sacrilegious in the States! What the British call a biscuit is something entirely different in America, more like a savory scone, which you might have with your eggs in the morning.

Regardless of whether you're making a snap or a cookie – or an Italian biscotti for that matter, like the one on page 65 – they all need to have a good level of flavor. I love a ginger snap (page 68), like the ones my mother used to make, but you really need to taste the ginger in there, so go big. With a cookie, you can also consider the texture in your final bake. The peanut butter cookies on page 62 have some great extra crunch going on from chopped salted peanuts mixed through the dough, contrasting with the slightly chewy cookie.

I think a traditional afternoon tea deserves a good scone. I've given you both my classic scone recipe and a cheese version (on pages 79 and 80) and I often serve one of each together. If you're looking for something more sophisticated, give the macarons a go – I've shared lime and chocolate versions on pages 76 and 74. They can be expensive to buy but they're really not difficult to make and use fairly basic ingredients; they just take a bit of patience.

A more savory choice would be the oatmeal crackers on page 70, which work well as part of a cheeseboard or topped with a piece of Stilton at the end of a meal. The cheese crackers on page 82 are delicious on their own, but they also make the perfect base for a canapé.

Finally, I feel I need to come back to the hot topic of dunking. I'm proud to say that I'm big on dunking. I dunk everything and I tend to judge a cookie on its dunkability. No one wants a cookie that can barely take a dunk before collapsing into and sitting at the bottom of your cup, so I can assure you that all the cookies in this chapter fully stand up to the dunk test.

Hazelnut and Apricot Cookies

Makes 10

Perfect with a cup of coffee, these cookies are deliciously chewy on the inside yet crisp on the outside, and dotted with pieces of sweet, dried apricots. The hazelnuts are blitzed and mixed into the flour which gives an even, nutty taste throughout and a slightly firmer texture.

Heaping ½ cup (50g) skinned hazelnuts

4 tbsp (60g) unsalted butter, softened

⅔ cup (125g) superfine sugar

1 large egg

1 cup (125g) all-purpose flour, plus extra to dust

1½ tsp baking powder

A pinch of fine salt

⅓ cup (40g) dried apricots, cut into bite-sized pieces

———

In a dry pan, toast the hazelnuts over a medium heat for a few minutes, until golden, stirring from time to time to ensure they color evenly. Remove from the heat. Tip the nuts into a food processor and blitz until finely ground.

In a large bowl, cream the butter and sugar together using an electric whisk until pale and fluffy. Add the egg and mix well. Sift the flour, baking powder and salt over the creamed mixture, add the ground hazelnuts and whisk slowly to mix in and form a stiff dough. Add the chopped apricots and mix until evenly incorporated.

Turn the dough out onto a lightly floured surface and knead it gently. Roll into a cylinder, 8 inches (20cm) long, and wrap in parchment paper or plastic wrap, sealing the ends. Chill for at least an hour.

Heat your oven to 350°F and line two large baking sheets with parchment paper.

Unwrap the dough and cut into 10 equal slices. Put on the prepared baking sheets, leaving plenty of space in between for them to spread. Bake for 12–15 minutes until golden – the cookies will still be soft when you take them from the oven.

Leave to cool on the baking sheets for a few minutes until firm, then transfer to a wire rack and leave to cool completely.

Double Chocolate Chip Cookies

Makes 16

Everyone loves a chewy chocolate chip cookie and baking them yourself means you get to enjoy them warm from the oven when the chocolate is still slightly melted. These use both bittersweet and milk chocolate, making them irresistible to adults and kids alike, but if you prefer you can use just one type, or swap some or all of the chocolate chips for white chocolate instead.

1 stick plus 2 tbsp (150g) butter, softened

¾ cup (150g) superfine sugar

½ cup (100g) light brown sugar

1 large egg

2 cups (250g) all-purpose flour

1 tsp baking powder

½ tsp fine salt

½ cup (45g) unsweetened cocoa powder

3 oz (75g) bittersweet chocolate, cut into chunks

⅓ cup (75g) milk chocolate chips

In a large bowl, cream the butter and sugars together using an electric whisk until smooth and fluffy. Add the egg and mix well.

Sift the flour with the baking powder, salt and cocoa powder over the creamed mixture and whisk slowly to mix and form a stiff dough. (At first, there will seem to be too much flour to incorporate but whisk slowly and a dough will form.)

Add the chocolate chunks along with the milk chocolate chips and knead gently to distribute evenly through the dough.

Tip onto a large sheet of parchment paper or plastic wrap and roll the dough into a cylinder, 11 inches (27cm) long and 2¼ inches (6cm) wide. Wrap in the parchment or plastic wrap and put in the fridge to firm up for at least 2 hours.

Heat your oven to 325°F and line two large baking sheets with parchment paper.

Unwrap the dough, cut into 16 equal slices and put on the prepared baking sheets, leaving space in between for them to spread. Bake for 12–15 minutes until the cookies have risen and spread out – they will still be soft when you take them from the oven.

Leave the cookies on the baking sheets for a few minutes to firm up before transferring them to a wire rack and leaving to cool completely.

Peanut Butter Cookies

Makes 16

Make a batch of this peanut butter cookie dough, keep it rolled and wrapped up in the fridge or freezer and you can cut off and cook slices whenever you fancy a freshly baked treat. Creamy peanut butter makes the dough easier to work with, while roughly chopped salted peanuts folded through add a bit of extra crunch.

1 stick plus 3 tbsp (160g) butter, softened

1 cup plus 2 tbsp (275g) creamy peanut butter

⅔ cup (135g) superfine sugar

⅔ cup (135g) light brown sugar

2 large eggs

2 cups (250g) all-purpose flour

1 tsp baking powder

½ tsp fine salt

½ cup (50g) salted peanuts, roughly chopped

In a large bowl, cream the butter, peanut butter and sugars together using an electric whisk until smooth and fluffy. Mix in the eggs, one at a time.

In another bowl, mix the flour with the baking powder, salt and chopped peanuts. Add to the butter mix and mix well to form a stiff dough.

Tip onto a large sheet of parchment paper or plastic wrap and roll the dough into a cylinder, 11 inches (28cm) long and 3½ inches (9cm) wide. Wrap in the parchment or plastic wrap and put in the fridge for at least 2 hours to firm up.

Heat your oven to 325°F and line two large baking sheets with parchment paper.

Unwrap the dough, cut into 16 equal slices and put on the prepared baking sheets. Bake for 14–16 minutes until the cookies are golden, risen and slightly cracked on the surface – they will still be soft when you remove them from the oven.

Leave the cookies to firm up on the baking sheets for a few minutes before transferring them to a wire rack to cool completely.

Almond and Orange Biscotti

Makes 18

Biscotti always remind me of my time in La Spezia in Liguria, learning to cook amazing Italian food. I'd have one of these with my morning cappuccino, looking out over the sea. They're perfect for dunking! Baking them twice – the second time after you have sliced the biscotti – is what gives them their famously crisp texture.

¾ cup (100g) raw almonds

¾ cup plus 1 tbsp (165g) superfine sugar

Finely grated zest of 1 orange

1⅓ cups (165g) all-purpose flour, plus extra to dust

½ tsp baking powder

A pinch of fine salt

2 large eggs

1 tsp orange extract

———

Heat your oven to 400°F and line two large baking sheets with parchment paper.

Scatter the almonds on a baking sheet and toast in the oven for 8 minutes, stirring a few times to prevent scorching. Tip onto a board, leave to cool then chop the nuts roughly.

Mix the sugar, orange zest, flour, baking powder and salt together in a bowl. Make a well in the center and add the eggs, orange extract and chopped almonds (**1**). Mix together until evenly combined to form a dough.

Turn the dough onto a lightly floured surface and divide in two. Form each into a log, about 9 inches (22cm) long, and press gently to flatten (**2**). Put the biscotti lengths on the prepared baking sheets (**3**). Bake for 20 minutes until golden brown.

Remove from the oven and lower the oven temperature to 300°F. Leave the biscotti logs to cool for 5 minutes, to firm up slightly.

Using a serrated knife, cut the biscotti logs on the diagonal into slices, about ½ inch (1cm) thick (**4**). Lay the slices on the baking sheets. Return to the oven and bake for 20 minutes until golden brown.

Transfer the biscotti to a wire rack and leave them to cool completely. Store in an airtight jar.

Steps illustrated overleaf

1

2

3

4

Ginger Snaps

Makes 18

My mother used to make fantastic ginger snaps when I was a kid and they've always been one of my favorites. We used to roll them into balls in our hands and flatten them down on a baking sheet with a fork. Within half an hour they'd be out of the oven and in the cookie jar – if they made it that far!

1¾ cups (225g) all-purpose flour

2 tsp ground ginger

½ tsp baking soda

7 tbsp (100g) butter, softened

½ cup (100g) superfine sugar

⅓ cup (100g) Lyle's golden syrup

Sift the flour, ginger and baking soda together into a large bowl. Add the butter, sugar and golden syrup and mix, using a hand-held electric whisk or wooden spoon, to form a smooth dough.

Wrap the dough in plastic wrap or parchment paper and chill in the fridge for about 30 minutes to firm up.

Heat your oven to 375°F. Line two large baking sheets with parchment paper.

Break off small pieces of dough, each about 1 heaping tablespoon (30g), and roll into balls. Put on the prepared baking sheets, leaving enough room for the cookies to spread. Bake for 10–12 minutes until they are golden with a cracked surface.

Leave the cookies to cool on the baking sheets for a few minutes until firm, then transfer to a wire rack to cool completely.

Oatmeal Crackers

Makes 10

5 tbsp (75g) unsalted butter

3 tbsp (50g) Lyle's golden syrup

¾ cup (90g) whole wheat flour

1 tsp baking powder

¾ cup plus 2 tbsp (90g) quick-cooking oats

¼ cup (50g) light brown sugar

These oatmeal crackers are great on their own, but I also like to serve them at the end of a meal with a good strong cheese. Their crumbly texture pairs beautifully with creamy Stilton.

———

Heat your oven to 350°F. Line one large (or two smaller) baking sheet(s) with parchment paper.

Melt the butter and golden syrup together in a small saucepan. In a large bowl, mix the flour, baking powder, oats and sugar together and make a well in the center. Pour in the melted mixture and mix until thoroughly combined to form a dough.

Divide the dough into 10 equal-sized pieces and roll into balls. Put on the baking sheet(s), spacing them well apart to allow for spreading.

Bake for 12–15 minutes until the crackers are golden brown. Leave to cool and firm up on the baking sheet(s) for 5 minutes, then transfer to a wire rack to cool completely.

Shortbread

Makes about 16

Shortbread is essentially a short crust, so it shouldn't be pummelled or kneaded for long. You only need to just fold the ingredients together, so the dough looks slightly smooth, then chill it in the fridge before you roll it out. Resting the dough in the fridge lets it sit back and relax, like it's in a big armchair, and gives the finished shortbread its lovely light, crumbly texture.

2 sticks (230g) unsalted butter, softened

½ cup plus 1 tbsp (110g) superfine sugar, plus extra to dust

2 cups (240g) all-purpose flour

¾ cup (80g) corn starch

A pinch of fine salt

Line two baking sheets with parchment paper.

In a large bowl, cream the butter and sugar together, using a hand-held electric whisk or wooden spoon, until light and fluffy.

Sift the flour and cornstarch together over the creamed mixture and add the salt. Mix together until smoothly combined and the dough starts to come together; be careful not to overwork it. Wrap the dough in parchment paper or plastic wrap and rest in the fridge for 30 minutes.

Roll out the dough between two sheets of parchment paper to a thickness of ½ inch (1cm), then remove the top sheet of paper.

Using a round cutter, about 2¼ inches (5½ cm) in diameter, or a sharp knife, cut out rounds or triangles and put on the lined baking sheets, leaving space in between. Prick with a fork. Re-roll any scraps (once, only) to cut more. Put in the fridge to rest for 15 minutes.

Meanwhile, heat your oven to 325°F. Bake the shortbreads for 15–20 minutes, until just turning golden brown at the edges.

Leave on the baking sheets for a few minutes to firm up slightly, then lift onto a wire rack. Dust with superfine sugar and leave to cool. Store the shortbreads in an airtight container; they will keep for 3–4 days.

Chocolate Macarons

Makes 32

An indulgent treat, but one made using fairly basic ingredients, macarons are a great foody gift. I still remember seeing them in Paris for the first time. They are stunning to look at but can be expensive to buy, so have a go at making them yourself. Take your time, be patient and enjoy the process.

_____

Chocolate macaron paste

3 large egg whites

2⅓ cups plus 1 tbsp (240g) almond flour

2⅓ cups plus 1 tbsp (240g) confectioners' sugar

5 tbsp (40g) unsweetened cocoa powder

Swiss meringue

3 large egg whites

1¼ cups (240g) superfine sugar

Chocolate filling

1¼ cups (300g) heavy cream

6 oz (150g) milk chocolate, chopped

4 oz (100g) bittersweet chocolate, chopped

2 tbsp (30g) butter, softened

First make the chocolate filling. Slowly bring the cream to a boil in a small saucepan. Put all the chocolate into a bowl and pour on the hot cream, stirring as you do so. Continue to stir until the chocolate is fully melted and smoothly combined. Add the butter and stir until incorporated. Set aside to cool and firm up.

Line four baking sheets with parchment paper. Using a biscuit cutter as a guide, draw circles, about 1¾ inches (4½cm) in diameter, on the paper, leaving a ¾-inch (2cm) gap between them. Turn the paper over and put on the baking sheet.

For the macaron paste, put the egg whites into a large bowl, add the almond flour and sift in the confectioners' sugar and cocoa powder. Mix to form a thick paste.

For the Swiss meringue, put the egg whites and sugar in a heatproof bowl and set over a saucepan of simmering water, making sure the base of the bowl is not in direct contact with the water. Using a balloon whisk, whisk until the sugar dissolves and the mixture reaches 150°F (use a candy thermometer to check). Now either transfer the mixture to a stand mixer fitted with the whisk attachment, or use an electric hand whisk to whisk the mixture until it has cooled and you have a stiff, glossy meringue – this will take at least 5 minutes.

Gradually fold the meringue into the chocolate macaron paste, a spoonful at a time (the mixture is stiff so this takes some effort).

Spoon into a paper pastry bag and snip off the end to create a ½-inch (1cm) opening (or use a pastry bag fitted with a ½-inch tip). Pipe the mixture evenly over the marked circles on the parchment paper. Leave to stand, uncovered, for at least 30 minutes, or until a skin forms. This helps prevent the surface from cracking.

Heat your oven to 300°F. Bake the macarons for 15 minutes, until risen and set. Leave to cool completely on the baking sheets before assembling.

To assemble, spoon the chocolate filling into a paper pastry bag and snip off the end. Pipe a little filling onto the center of half the macaron discs, leaving a narrow margin around the edge. Sandwich together with the remaining macaron discs.

Lime Macarons

Makes 30

Lime is one of my favorite flavors and I think it works really well with the almond in these macarons, but you can use whatever filling you like – apricot purée or cherry preserves are great choices, or you can replace the lime zest and juice with orange or lemon.

———

Macaron paste

3 large egg whites

2¾ cups (275g) almond flour

2¾ cups (275g) confectioners' sugar

Swiss meringue

3 large egg whites

1¼ cups (240g) superfine sugar

A few drops of green food coloring

Lime filling

1 stick plus 4 tbsp (175g) unsalted butter, softened

4¾ cups (475g) confectioners' sugar, sifted

Finely grated zest of 1 lime and 2 tbsp juice

Line three baking sheets with parchment paper. Using a biscuit cutter as a guide, draw circles, 1¾ inches (4½cm) in diameter, on the paper, leaving a ¾-inch (2cm) gap between them. Turn the paper over and put on the baking sheet.

For the macaron paste, put the egg whites into a large bowl, add the almond flour and then sift in the confectioners' sugar. Mix together to form a thick paste.

For the Swiss meringue, put the egg whites and sugar in a heatproof bowl and set over a saucepan of simmering water, making sure the base of the bowl is not in direct contact with the water. Using a balloon whisk, whisk until the sugar dissolves and the mixture reaches 150°F (use a candy thermometer to check). Now either transfer the mixture to a stand mixer fitted with the whisk attachment, or use an electric hand whisk to whisk the mixture until it has cooled and you have a stiff, glossy meringue – this will take at least 5 minutes.

Gradually fold the meringue into the macaron paste, a spoonful at a time, until fully incorporated. Add the coloring and mix until evenly combined.

Spoon the mixture into a paper pastry bag and snip off the end to create a ½-inch (1cm) opening (or use a pastry bag fitted with a plain tip of this size). Pipe the mixture evenly over the marked circles on the parchment paper. Leave the macarons to stand, uncovered, for at least 30 minutes, or until a skin forms. This helps prevent the surface from cracking.

Heat your oven to 300°F. Bake the macarons for 15 minutes, until risen and set. Leave to cool completely on the baking sheets before assembling.

To make the filling, using an electric hand whisk, beat the butter until soft then beat in the confectioners' sugar, a few spoonfuls at a time. Add the lime zest and juice and whisk again. Put in a paper pastry bag and snip off the end.

To assemble, pipe a little lime filling onto the center of half the macaron discs, leaving a narrow margin around the edge. Sandwich these together with the remaining macaron discs.

Classic Scones

I use bread flour in my scones which might seem surprising, but it's actually a popular choice in professional kitchens because the high protein content gives the scones a real boost. This recipe is tried and tested over many years and I've never had any complaints. The Queen Mother even said they were the best scones she'd ever tasted! Just a couple of things to bear in mind: don't overwork the dough, you want it nice and light, and don't twist the cutter when you lift it off or else they won't rise properly in the oven.

4 cups (500g) bread flour, plus extra to dust

2 tbsp (25g) baking powder

6 tbsp (80g) unsalted butter, cut into pieces

2 large eggs

1 cup (250g) whole milk

⅓ cup (80g) superfine sugar

To glaze

1 large egg, beaten with a pinch of salt

To serve

Confectioners' sugar, to dust

Preserves and Devonshire clotted cream or whipped cream

Line two baking sheets with parchment paper.

In a large bowl, mix the flour and baking powder together. Add the butter and rub together with your fingers for a few minutes until you have a breadcrumb-like texture.

In another bowl, beat the eggs with the milk and sugar. Add to the rubbed-in mixture and stir together until the dough comes together and forms a ball.

Tip the dough onto a lightly floured surface and fold it over a few times to incorporate air, but do not knead it; you want to achieve a loose, soft dough. Using a rolling pin, gently roll out to a 1¼-inch (3cm) thickness, making sure there is plenty of flour underneath to prevent sticking.

Using a biscuit cutter, about 2½ inches (6½cm) in diameter, and pressing firmly (without twisting the cutter), cut out rounds and put on the lined baking sheets, leaving space in between. Brush the tops of the scones with beaten egg then put in the fridge for 20 minutes to rest.

Meanwhile, heat your oven to 425°F.

Take the scones out of the fridge and brush them again with the egg glaze. Bake for 15 minutes until risen and golden brown.

Transfer the scones to a wire rack and leave to cool completely. Dust lightly with confectioners' sugar and serve with a generous helping of preserves and Devonshire clotted cream or whipped cream.

Cheese Scones

Makes 8

I love cheese scones, possibly even more than classic scones. I had to include them in this book because they're one of my absolute favorite things to eat. These have melted Cheddar inside and grated Parmesan on top, and they're incredible still warm from the oven with a little butter. I also like to serve them as part of an afternoon tea – alongside a plate of classic scones so people can choose either... or try both.

———

2 cups (250g) bread flour

½ tsp fine salt

2 tbsp (25g) baking powder

3 tbsp (40g) butter, cut into pieces

1 large egg

7 tbsp (110g) milk

1½ cups (150g) grated Cheddar

To glaze and finish

1 large egg, beaten with a pinch of salt

½ cup (50g) freshly grated Parmesan

Heat your oven to 425°F and line a large baking sheet with parchment paper.

In a large bowl, mix the flour, salt and baking powder together. Add the butter and rub together with your fingers for a few minutes until the mixture has a breadcrumb-like texture.

In another bowl, beat the egg with the milk, then add to the rubbed-in mixture with the grated cheese and gently fold together to form a loose paste; do not overwork it. Tip onto a lightly floured surface and fold over a couple of times to form a smooth, soft dough.

Using a rolling pin, gently roll out the soft dough to a 1-inch (2½cm) thickness and cut out rounds using a biscuit cutter, about 2½ inches (6½cm) in diameter, pressing firmly and avoiding twisting the cutter. Put them on the lined baking sheet, leaving space in between.

Brush the tops of the scones with beaten egg and sprinkle generously with Parmesan. Bake for 15 minutes until risen and golden brown. Transfer to a wire rack to cool.

Cheese Crackers

Makes 20

It's all about the bake with these simple Gruyère and Parmesan cheese crackers. There's a lot of butter in the dough, so don't bring them out of the oven too early or they'll be soggy. Let them take on a bit of color, which will give a good texture when you bite into them. They are delicious on their own, or as a canapé topped with Brie and sliced grapes. Feel free to play with the shape too.

1 cup plus 2 tbsp (150g) all-purpose flour, plus extra to dust

A pinch of fine salt

1 stick plus 2 tbsp (150g) unsalted butter, diced

1½ cups (150g) shredded Gruyère

1 large egg, beaten, to glaze

¾ cup (80g) freshly grated Parmesan

Cracked black pepper

Put the flour and salt into a large bowl, add the butter and rub in with your fingers for about 30 seconds. Add the shredded Gruyère and continue to rub the mixture for a minute or two until it comes together and forms a ball. Transfer the dough to a lightly floured surface and fold a few times, then put in a freezer bag and chill for 30 minutes.

Heat your oven to 400°F and line two baking sheets with parchment paper. Divide the dough in half to make it easier to roll out.

On a lightly floured surface, roll out each portion of dough thinly, until about ⅛ inch (3mm) thick. Using a pastry cutter, no bigger than 2¾ inches (7cm), cut out discs or other shapes and put on the prepared baking sheets. Brush the top of each one lightly with beaten egg, then sprinkle with the Parmesan and a little cracked pepper.

Bake for 10–15 minutes until the crackers are lightly browned. Leave the crackers to cool and firm up on the baking sheet.

2

3

4

Breads and Flatbreads

There is a wonderful tactile element to making bread and it's a skill that you can really get better at and master. Working with a rudimentary dough of flour, salt, yeast and water, it's just incredible how many different breads you can produce.

Breads have always been my passion, and I think it's in part because bread tells such an incredible story about us as humans. At the heart of almost every culture in the world, you'll find a bread of some form. As we moved around the world and settled in different locations, we took our key recipes with us. Sourdough bread, with its distinctive open structure and slightly acidic flavor, may go in and out of fashion, but it has a truly amazing heritage. Traces of the yeasts used to make sourdough have even been found around the Pyramids of Giza, dating back to 4,500 BC.

You can try my version of sourdough on page 121, using the same age-old techniques but baking in a very modern oven. Loaves like this were usually cooked in large clay pots or in a brick oven. Other, more nomadic cultures needed breads which could be easily transported and only required basic, lightweight tools. That's where flatbreads, like tortillas, maneesh and chapatis came about (see pages 149, 146 and 150 respectively). Cooked over an open fire, they were simple to make and lasted well on journeys.

From a basic soda bread (page 114) that you can make in under an hour, to a traditional baguette, Greek pita, sweet orange brioche and iced finger buns (see pages 102, 144, 132 and 130 respectively), there is a bread for every occasion and every skill level. If you're new to making bread, I suggest you start out with one of the classic sandwich loaves – the white sandwich loaf on page 92 or the whole wheat version on page 96. A great sandwich is a joy to eat and it all starts with a good slice of bread. For a more formal tea, I'd make egg and sprouts, beef and mustard, cucumber or smoked salmon sandwiches – sliced thinly with the crusts cut off. Beautiful. Otherwise, I'm a big fan of ham, cucumber, tomato and a smear of salad cream or mayonnaise.

If you're going to the effort of making bread, then it's often worth making two at a time and keeping one in the freezer. That's why many of the recipes in this chapter give instructions for two loaves. Bread freezes well and thaws in a couple of hours, so I usually make two of everything. If you'd rather make just one loaf, then you can easily halve the recipe quantities.

The fundamentals of bread-making are simple, so enjoy the process and learn as you go. There's nothing more satisfying than making your own bread and I promise that once you start, it will change your life.

The key stages of bread-making

1 Mixing and kneading

First you need to mix your ingredients together to form a dough and then you need to work that dough to develop the gluten in the flour. This gives it structure and helps it to rise. Add the salt and yeast to opposite sides of the bowl, as direct contact between the two can kill off the yeast. Flours vary in the amount of liquid they absorb, so add it slowly, to ensure you get the right amount.

A stand mixer fitted with a paddle or dough hook attachment makes lighter work of a long knead and I recommend using a mixer for wet doughs, such as ciabatta and brioche. Others, like flatbreads, I suggest you make by hand, as the dough is so simple and quick. If you're kneading by hand, use the heel of your hand to stretch the dough away, then fold it over, rotate it and repeat. And knead for longer than you think you should! Thorough kneading will produce a better loaf. Whether you're using a mixer or doing it by hand, the dough is ready when it has a soft, smooth, elastic consistency and comes away from the side of the bowl. Avoid using too much extra flour when you knead, as it will change the recipe.

2 Rising

You can't rush this stage. Most people's homes are around 70°F, which is a great temperature for dough to rise so you don't need to put it in a warmer place. Cover the bowl with plastic wrap or a clean kitchen towel, so there are no cold drafts, and it will grow beautifully. The yeast produces carbon dioxide which forms bubbles in the dough, and this is what gives it its rise. Properly working the dough beforehand so it's nice and stretchy will help it double in size.

3 Knocking back and shaping

This is a crucial stage in the process and one that comes down to practice. If you don't knock the air pockets out of the risen dough and then reshape it with the palm of your hand, it will collapse and flow all over the baking sheet in the oven. Although it seems counter-intuitive to knock the air out of the dough, it will help it rise evenly and keep its shape as it bakes. Use the heel of your hand to knock it down, fold it over to build up resistance and then shape it with the palm of your hand nice and gently, tucking it underneath to give some tension to the outside.

4 Proofing

I usually put my knocked-back and shaped dough in a reusable freezer bag for this stage. You can put the dough on a baking sheet and put the baking sheet into the bag, making sure you leave room for the dough to rise so it doesn't come into contact with the bag.

5 Baking

The baking time and temperature can hugely impact the final look and feel of your bread. Sweeter breads usually have shorter cooking times to ensure they retain their moisture inside and stay soft. Whereas heavier loaves tend to need longer in the oven to get a good strong crust. Generally, you're after a crisp crust and a soft interior. Take the loaf out of the oven and give it a tap on the base. You want it to sound hollow; if it doesn't, cook it for a further 5 minutes.

White Sandwich Bread

Makes 2 loaves

This is the bread I make most often. I usually have one of these loaves in the bread box and one stashed in the freezer. It's such a versatile, go-to loaf, perfect for toast and sandwiches and a great way to get into baking bread. Simply halve the quantities if you want to make one loaf.

6⅓ cups (800g) bread flour, plus extra to dust

1¾ tsp (14g) fine salt

1 x ¼-oz (7g) envelope instant dried yeast

1 tbsp plus 1 tsp (20g) olive oil, plus extra for oiling

About 2½ cups (600g) cool water

———

Combine all the ingredients in a large bowl and stir together for a minute to form a dough (see page 90). Tip onto a lightly oiled surface and knead well for 10–15 minutes until the dough is soft and elastic (**1**). Alternatively, use a stand mixer fitted with the dough hook to mix and knead the dough, for 3–4 minutes on slow and 10 minutes on medium speed.

Put the dough back in the bowl, cover the bowl with plastic wrap and leave to rise at room temperature for 2 hours.

Lightly oil two 1-pound (500g) loaf pans. Tip the dough out onto a lightly floured surface (**2**) and knock back by folding it inwards repeatedly until all the air is knocked out. Divide the dough in half (**3**).

Flatten out each piece into a rectangle and fold the sides into the middle. Then starting at the top, flatten it slightly and roll it up. Ensure the seam is underneath and neaten the sides by tucking them under (**4**).

Put the dough in the prepared loaf pans and dust with flour. Using a sharp knife, score the top of each loaf, along its length. Put each pan inside a roomy freezer bag. Leave to proof at room temperature for about 2 hours until at least doubled in size.

Heat your oven to 415°F. Bake the loaves for 35 minutes or until cooked; to check, tip a loaf out of the pan and tap the base – it should sound hollow. Leave to cool, out of the pan, on a wire rack.

Once cooled, the extra loaf can be frozen in a freezer bag. It will take 1–2 hours to thaw at room temperature.

Steps illustrated overleaf

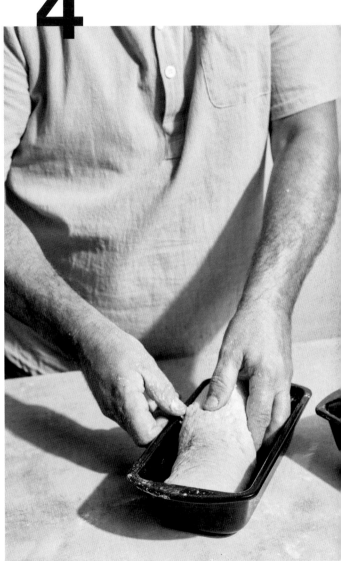

Stoneground Whole Wheat Sandwich Bread

Makes 2 loaves

Make sure you use proper stoneground whole wheat flour for this loaf as that's where all the flavor is. Whole wheat flour produces a denser dough than white flour, so if you want to ease yourself into eating whole wheat bread you could start with a 50/50 blend with bread flour and gradually increase the proportion of whole wheat as you get used to it. You can make this bread by hand, but I'd recommend using a stand mixer if you have one. Halve the quantities if you want to make just one loaf.

6⅓ cups (800g) stoneground whole wheat bread flour, plus extra to dust

1¾ tsp (14g) fine salt

1 x ¼-oz (7g) envelope instant dried yeast

1 tbsp plus 1 tsp (20g) honey

1 tbsp plus 1 tsp (20g) olive oil, plus extra for oiling

About 2½ cups (600g) cool water

¾ cup plus 1 tbsp (80g) quick-cookng oats

Combine all the ingredients, except the oats, in a large bowl and stir together for a minute to form a dough (see page 90). Tip onto a lightly oiled surface and knead well for 10–15 minutes until the dough is soft and elastic. Alternatively, use a stand mixer fitted with the dough hook to mix and knead the dough, for 3–4 minutes on slow and 10 minutes on medium speed.

Put the dough back in the bowl, cover the bowl with plastic wrap and leave to rise at room temperature for 2 hours.

Lightly oil two 1-pound (500g) loaf pans. Tip the dough out onto a lightly floured surface and fold it inwards repeatedly until all the air is knocked out. Divide the dough in half.

Flatten out each piece into a rectangle and fold the sides into the middle. Then starting at the top, flatten slightly and roll up. Ensure the seam is underneath and neaten the sides by tucking them under.

Brush the top of each loaf with water then roll in the oats. Put in the prepared loaf pans and put each inside a freezer bag. Leave to proof at room temperature for 2 hours until at least doubled in size.

Heat your oven to 415°F. Bake the loaves for 35 minutes or until cooked; to check, tip a loaf out of the pan and tap the base – it should sound hollow. Leave to cool, out of the pan, on a wire rack.

Once cooled, the extra loaf can be frozen in a freezer bag. It will take 1–2 hours to thaw at room temperature.

Ciabatta

Makes 2 large or
3–4 smaller loaves

The high water content of ciabatta dough makes it very soft to work with, but it is essential for creating a good open structure in the final bake. The trick is to drip in the final quarter of the liquid very slowly, once the dough is fully developed. It's all about taking your time with ciabatta to create a beautiful, elastic, silky dough. You really need to use a stand mixer for this one, as the dough is very wet and sticky to handle.

4 cups (500g) bread flour, plus extra to dust

Scant 1 tsp (7g) fine salt

1¾ tsp (5g) instant dried yeast

About 1⅔ cups (400g) cool water

Olive oil, for oiling

Put the flour, salt, yeast and three-quarters of the water into a stand mixer fitted with the dough hook and mix on slow speed for 3 minutes. Slowly increase the speed to medium and mix for 5 minutes; your dough should now be well formed. With the motor running, slowly add the remaining water over 2 minutes.

Continue to mix on medium speed for at least 15 minutes until the dough is elastic and glossy. To check the dough is ready, rip off a little bit and stretch it out; it should expand easily to form a webbing of gluten. If it's difficult to stretch, continue to mix for another 2–3 minutes.

Put the dough in a well-oiled 2-quart (2-liter) square or rectangular plastic container and leave to rise until at least doubled in size; this should take 2–3 hours.

Line two baking sheets with parchment paper. When the dough is well risen, heavily dust your work surface with flour and slowly tip the dough onto it. Sprinkle the surface of the dough with plenty of flour too. Tap the dough into a rough rectangle. Using a bench scraper (or floured sharp knife), cut the dough into two lengths, each about 5 inches (12cm) wide (or into 3 or 4 lengths for smaller loaves).

Carefully lift the ciabatta onto the baking sheets, stretching each one lengthwise as you do so, to fit the length of your baking sheets; position them so the cutting marks are on top of the dough.

Put each baking sheet into a freezer bag and leave the dough to proof for another 30 minutes. Heat your oven to 400°F.

Put your ciabattas into the oven and spray the oven with plenty of water as you do so. Bake for 30 minutes, or until risen and golden brown, and the loaves sound hollow when tapped on the base. Transfer to a wire rack to cool.

Baguettes

Makes 4

Baguettes are one of my favorite breads, reminding me of holidays in France, waking up and wandering down to the boulangerie to pick up a fresh loaf, still crispy and warm from the oven. All you need is good butter and good preserves for the perfect breakfast. The long proof is when all the flavor is introduced so take your time with it. A special perforated curved half-baguette pan will help give you a perfect shape, but otherwise you can use a regular baking sheet.

6⅓ cups (800g) bread flour, plus extra to dust

Scant 1 tsp (7g) fine salt

¾ tsp (2g) instant dried yeast

About 2½ cups (600g) cool water

———

Combine all the ingredients in a large bowl and stir for 30 seconds or so to form a dough (see page 90). Tip onto a lightly oiled surface and knead well for 5–8 minutes until the dough is soft and elastic. Alternatively, use a stand mixer fitted with the dough hook to mix and knead the dough, for 4 minutes on slow and 6 minutes on medium speed.

Cover the bowl with plastic wrap and leave to rise at room temperature for 7 hours. The mixture should at least double in size.

Tip the dough out onto a lightly floured surface. Fold the edges into the middle, then rotate the dough 90° and repeat. Continue folding and rotating the dough for about 5 minutes until the dough is smooth and glossy. Return to the bowl.

Cover the bowl with plastic wrap and leave the dough to rise at room temperature for a further hour.

Tip the dough out onto a lightly floured surface and divide into 4 equal pieces. Flatten one piece into a rough rectangle and fold the sides into the middle. With a long side facing you, fold the long edge furthest from you firmly into the middle and roll up tightly. Repeat with the other 3 pieces of dough. You should now have 4 sausage-shaped dough pieces.

Have ready a perforated half-baguette pan, or use one or two large baking sheets. Roll each dough sausage out to the length of your pan and taper the ends before putting on the pan.

Put the pan in a roomy freezer bag and leave to proof at room temperature for 5–6 hours (or overnight in the fridge, bringing the dough back to room temperature before baking).

Continued overleaf

Heat your oven to 400°F and put a small baking sheet at the bottom of your oven to heat up.

Using a very sharp knife or a blade, score 3 lines along the length of each baguette, on the diagonal. Leave to rest for 15 minutes before baking.

Put the pan(s) of baguettes in the middle of the oven and spray them and the inside of the oven with water as you do so; also, put a handful of ice cubes into the lower baking sheet. Bake for 20–25 minutes until the loaves are a rich golden-brown color. Leave them to cool in the pan.

Because the baguettes have no added fat in the dough they will harden within a day. My advice is to freeze any you're not going to eat straight away once they have cooled. Leave to thaw at room temperature then put the baguettes in an oven heated to 425°F for 5 minutes to refresh.

Pain de Campagne

Makes 1 large loaf

A classic bread that screams of French baking, the secret to this loaf is the little bit of rye flour in the mix and the long rise, which gives the bread its amazing flavor and texture. Rye flour is very fine, almost like talcum powder, and it can be a bit tricky to work with if you're not used to it, so I've blended it with bread flour here. The longer bake produces a rich, strong, caramelized crust that splinters beautifully as you slice it.

6 cups (750g) bread flour, plus extra to dust

⅓ cup plus 1 tbsp (50g) rye flour

1¾ tsp (14g) fine salt

¾ tsp (2g) instant dried yeast

About 2½ cups (600g) cool water

In a large bowl, combine the flours, salt and yeast. Pour in the water and stir with a wooden spoon for about 30 seconds or so to form a dough (see page 90). Tip out onto a lightly oiled surface and knead well for 10–15 minutes until the dough is soft and elastic. Alternatively, use a stand mixer fitted with the dough hook to mix and knead the dough, for 3–4 minutes on slow and 10–12 minutes on medium speed.

Cover the bowl with a large freezer bag and leave the dough to rise at room temperature for 7–8 hours.

Tip the dough out onto a lightly floured surface and fold it inwards repeatedly until all the air is knocked out. Now shape into a round by gently tucking your hands underneath the dough and rotating it. After a minute or so, tension will be formed on the top and the dough will be smooth and shaped into a ball.

Put the ball of dough, smooth side up, in a floured banneton or on a heavily floured cloth. Cover and leave to rise for a further 2–3 hours until doubled in size.

Heat your oven to 425°F and put a pizza stone on the middle shelf to heat up for at least an hour. Put a roasting pan on a lower shelf to heat up too (for 20 minutes or so).

Carefully turn the risen dough out of the banneton or lift it off the cloth onto a floured peel. Using a very sharp blade or knife, score a deep cross on the top of the dough.

Using the peel, carefully transfer the dough to the hot pizza stone and pour about 2 cups (500g) water into the hot pan below (to create steam in the oven). Bake for 50 minutes or until the loaf is deep golden brown and sounds hollow when tapped on the base. Transfer to a wire rack to cool.

Seeded Sandwich Bread

Makes 2 loaves

This is a bit of a health-kick of a loaf from the poppy, pumpkin, sunflower, caraway and sesame seeds, which also give it an amazing taste and texture. A fairly dense bread, it's great toasted with cheese or simply sliced with butter; the crusty bit at the end is particularly good. It's quite unusual for me to use white, rye and whole wheat flours together but it gives a real intensity of flavor and a fantastic color. Halve the quantities if you'd rather make one loaf.

———

Dough

3¼ cups (400g) bread flour, plus extra to dust

2¾ cups (350g) stoneground whole wheat flour

⅓ cup plus 1 tbsp (50g) rye flour

1¾ tsp (14g) fine salt

1 x ¼-oz (7g) envelope instant dried yeast

1 tbsp plus 1 tsp (20g) honey

1 tbsp plus 1 tsp (20g) olive oil, plus extra for oiling

About 3 cups (700g) cool water

Seed mix

½ cup (80g) poppy seeds

½ cup (80g) pumpkin seeds

½ cup (80g) sunflower seeds

2 tbsp (20g) caraway seeds

Topping

⅔ cup (100g) white sesame seeds

Combine all the ingredients for the dough in a large bowl and stir together for a minute to form a dough (see page 90). Tip onto a lightly oiled surface and knead well for 10–15 minutes until the dough is soft and elastic. Alternatively, use a stand mixer fitted with the dough hook to mix and knead the dough, for 3–4 minutes on slow and 10 minutes on medium speed.

Put the dough back in the bowl, cover the bowl with plastic wrap and leave to rise for 1 hour.

Tip the dough out onto a lightly floured surface and fold it inwards repeatedly until all the air is knocked out. Flatten the dough slightly. Scatter the poppy, pumpkin, sunflower and caraway seeds on top and knead to distribute them evenly through the dough. Put back in the bowl, re-cover and leave to rise for a further 1½ hours.

Lightly oil two 1-pound (500g) loaf pans. Tip the dough out onto a lightly floured surface, knock back again to exclude the air and divide in half. Flatten out each piece into a rectangle and fold the sides into the middle. Then starting at the top, flatten slightly and roll up. Ensure the seam is underneath and neaten the sides by tucking them under.

Brush the top of each loaf with water then roll in the sesame seeds. Put the loaves in the prepared loaf pans. Put each pan inside a roomy freezer bag and leave to proof at room temperature for 2 hours until at least doubled in size.

Heat your oven to 415°F. Bake the loaves for 35 minutes or until cooked; to check, tip a loaf out of the pan and tap the base – it should sound hollow. Leave to cool, out of the pan, on a wire rack.

Once cooled, the extra loaf can be frozen in a freezer bag. It will take 1–2 hours to thaw at room temperature.

Cheesy Bread

Makes 1 large loaf

I think cheese in bread is a real winner. This loaf is flavored with sharp Cheddar, Parmesan and Brie or Camembert and when you smell it in the oven, you'll never want to stop baking it! The idea is to ram as much cheese in there as possible to create an extremely enriched dough. Be careful not to overwork the dough though, because you want to taste little chunks of cheese in the final loaf. It takes a little while to rise due to the amount of cheese, so you'll need to allow for this. I enjoy it with soup in the winter and with salad in the summer.

———

Dough

6⅓ cups (800g) bread flour

1¾ tsp (14g) fine salt

¾ tsp (2g) instant dried yeast

About 2½ cups (600g) cool water

A little oil, for oiling

Filling

2 cups (200g) grated sharp Cheddar

7 oz (200g) Brie or Camembert, in small pieces

1 cup (100g) freshly grated Parmesan

In a large bowl, combine the dough ingredients and mix, using one hand or a wooden spoon, for 1 minute to form a dough (see page 90). Tip onto a lightly oiled surface and knead well for about 10 minutes until the dough is soft and elastic. Alternatively, use a stand mixer fitted with the dough hook to mix and knead the dough, for 3–4 minutes on slow and 10 minutes on medium speed.

Cover the bowl with a large freezer bag and leave to rise at room temperature for 6 hours.

Oil an 8-inch (20cm) springform pan well. Tip the dough out onto a lightly oiled surface and fold it inwards repeatedly until all the air is knocked out. Flatten the dough slightly and scatter over the grated Cheddar and Brie or Camembert, along with half of the Parmesan. Knead until the filling is well distributed.

Gently tuck the dough underneath and rotate to create tension on the top. Turn the dough 90° and repeat. Continue to shape the dough in this way until you have a smooth round.

Put the dough in the prepared springform pan. Put the pan inside a roomy freezer bag and leave to proof at room temperature for 6 hours. Your dough should now be well risen.

Heat your oven to 400°F. Spray the dough with water and sprinkle with the remaining Parmesan. Using a sharp knife, cut a cross in the top of the loaf. Bake for 1 hour until golden brown. Remove the loaf from the pan and cool on a wire rack.

Cheese and Onion Soda Bread

Makes 2 loaves

Soda bread is a great place to start if you've never baked bread before. Instead of yeast, baking soda and buttermilk give the dough its lift, so there's no need to wait for it to proof as you do with other breads. You can even set yourself your own little baking challenge with this cheese and onion version, as you can make it well within the hour. If you've got guests arriving at short notice you can still bake a fresh loaf that will wow everyone, and your kitchen will smell amazing.

¾ cup (100g) whole wheat flour

3¼ cups (400g) all-purpose flour, plus extra to dust

1 tsp fine salt

1 tsp baking soda

1⅔ cups (400g) buttermilk

1½ cups (150g) grated Cheddar

½ onion, diced and sautéed in a little oil to soften

A little milk, to brush

1 cup (100g) freshly grated Parmesan

Heat your oven to 400°F. Have ready two baking sheets.

Combine the flours, salt and baking soda in a large bowl. Add the buttermilk and mix together, using one hand, to form a sticky dough. Gently fold the dough to bring it together for a couple of minutes; it should feel soft.

Add the grated cheese and sautéed onion to the dough and fold to incorporate evenly. Tip the dough out onto a lightly floured surface and fold again for a minute, then divide in half.

Shape each portion of dough into a ball, using the heel of your hand, and put on a baking sheet. Using a sharp knife, cut a deep cross in each loaf. Brush the top of each loaf with a little milk and sprinkle with the Parmesan.

Bake for 30 minutes or until the loaves are golden brown and sound hollow when tapped on the base. Transfer to a wire rack to cool.

Soda bread is best eaten on the day it is made, but you can keep it in the bread box for a day or two. It also freezes well, so I usually freeze the second loaf. Let thaw at room temperature then put the loaf in an oven heated to 400°F for 4–5 minutes to refresh.

Barm Cakes

Makes 13

Barm cakes are soft white rolls that originated in north-west England and I think they are very underrated. My father used to bring them back from the bakery and we would eat them with a little butter and some good ham. They're perfect for burgers, too. The secret to a quality barm cake is to let it proof for long enough to ensure the end result is nice and light. And don't overcook them – as soon as they show a little bit of light brown color on top, take them out of the oven.

4 cups (500g) bread flour, plus extra to dust

3 tbsp (40g) lard or vegetable shortening

1¼ tsp (10g) fine salt

3 tbsp (40g) superfine sugar

1 x ¼-oz (7g) envelope instant dried yeast

About 1 cup plus 2 tbsp (280g) cool water

———

Put the flour into a large bowl and rub in the lard or vegetable shortening with your fingers, then stir in the salt, sugar and yeast. Pour in the water and stir to combine and form a dough that comes together in a ball (see page 90). Tip the dough onto a lightly floured surface and knead well for 10 minutes. Alternatively, use a stand mixer fitted with the dough hook to mix and knead the dough, for 2 minutes on slow and 7 minutes on medium speed.

Put the dough back in the bowl, cover with a freezer bag and leave to rise at room temperature for 1½ hours.

Tip the dough out onto a lightly floured surface and fold it inwards repeatedly until all the air is knocked out. Divide the dough into 13 balls, each about ¼ cup (60g). Flatten each ball slightly to form a round, put on a well-floured surface and leave to rest for 10 minutes.

Line two or three large baking sheets with parchment paper.

Using a floured rolling pin, roll each dough piece out to a larger round, about 4 inches (10cm) in diameter. Put the rolls on the prepared baking sheets, leaving plenty of space in between for them to rise, and dust the tops lightly with flour.

Put each baking sheet in a roomy freezer bag and leave the rolls to proof at room temperature for 1½ hours until doubled in size.

Heat your oven to 415°F. Bake the rolls for 10 minutes or until golden. Leave them to cool on the baking sheets. Once cooled, the barm cakes can be frozen.

Bin Lids

Makes 4

A bin lid is the British term for a trash can lid and these rolls resemble their shape. Growing up in north-west England, we used to make huge sandwiches with these – we'd tip a whole bag of fish and chips into the middle of a bin lid for a real treat! The dough contains a little sugar and egg, so it's slightly enriched, but simple to make. Fill them with whatever you want and then divide them up – but if you want to make a proper British "chip butty", this is the one.

4 cups (500g) bread flour, plus extra to dust

1¼ tsp (10g) fine salt

1 x ¼-oz (7g) envelope instant dried yeast

3 tbsp (40g) superfine sugar

3 tbsp (40g) lard or vegetable shortening

1 large egg, beaten

About scant 1 cup (220g) cool water

Combine all of the ingredients in a large bowl and stir well to form a smooth dough that comes together in a ball (see page 90). Tip out onto a lightly floured surface and knead well for 10 minutes. Alternatively, use a stand mixer fitted with the dough hook to mix and knead the dough, for 2 minutes on slow and 7 minutes on medium speed.

Put the dough back in the bowl, cover with a freezer bag and leave to rise at room temperature for 2 hours.

Tip the dough out onto a lightly floured surface and fold it inwards repeatedly until all the air is knocked out. Divide into 4 pieces and roll each piece into a ball. Leave to rest on a well-floured surface for 10 minutes.

Line two large baking sheets with parchment paper. Using a floured rolling pin, roll each dough ball out to a round, 7 inches (18cm) in diameter. Put the dough rounds on the prepared baking sheets, leaving plenty of space in between for them to rise. Dust them with flour.

Put each baking sheet in a large freezer bag and leave to proof at room temperature for 1½ hours until doubled in size.

Heat your oven to 415°F. Bake the rolls for 15 minutes or until golden. Leave to cool on the baking sheets.

Sourdough

Makes 1 loaf

Sourdough has one of the oldest bread-making traditions in the world. The flavor is amazing – earthy, strong and punchy – and it has a fantastic heavy crust and open structure inside. There are quite a few stages to the process because you're effectively making your own yeast from flour and water, called a 'starter'. And then you have to feed and look after your starter, which is a bit like looking after a pet! Once you get the hang of making sourdough though, it will change your life. This bread also benefits from using a banneton, which is a specially designed bowl to help the dough keep its shape while rising.

──────

Starter
¾ cup (100g) bread flour
7 tbsp (100ml) tepid water

To feed the starter (each time)
½ cup (60g) bread flour
¼ cup (60g) tepid water

Dough
3⅔ cups (450g) bread flour,
plus extra to dust
1¼ tsp (10g) fine sea salt
1⅓ cups (320g) tepid water
⅔ cup (150g) sourdough starter
A little oil, for oiling

To prepare the starter

Day 1 Using a fork, mix the flour and water together in a bowl to form a smooth paste. Transfer to a large jar, seal and leave at warm room temperature (ideally 68–75°F) to ferment over the next 2 days. The mixture should start to froth up.

Day 3 Open the jar: there should be a distinctive light vinegary (not unpleasant) aroma. Discard half of the mixture then add ½ cup (60g) flour and ¼ cup (60g) tepid water and stir together until no flour can be seen. Seal the jar again and leave to ferment again for 24 hours.

Day 4 Your starter should be risen and forming bubbles now – within the 24 hours. Throw away half of the mixture and feed with another ½ cup (60g) flour and ¼ cup (60g) water. Stir together as before, re-seal and leave to rise again overnight.

Day 5 You should have an active starter now, with bubbles on the top and throughout. This indicates that it is ready to use. If there are few bubbles and/or the starter appears to have risen and fallen (marks on the side of the jar suggest this), your starter is inactive and you will need to feed it again, as on day 4, to stimulate fermentation.

Storing and using your starter

Once your starter is active, you will need to feed it (as above) after each use. If you bake regularly, keep it at room temperature. If you bake infrequently, keep the jar in the fridge to slow down the starter's activity. A brown liquid may form on the top while it is in the fridge; discard this and feed with more flour and water (as above). You will know when your starter is ready to use because once you've fed it, it will bubble up and double in size within 6 hours.

Continued overleaf

To prepare the dough

Put the flour, salt and tepid water in a stand mixer fitted with the dough hook and mix on a slow speed for 4–5 minutes. Increase the speed to medium and mix for a further 10 minutes. Add the starter and mix on a slow speed for 1 minute, then on medium speed for a further 15 minutes. Your dough should be soft and elastic: open a small piece to see the structure – it should hold together well.

Put the dough in an oiled bowl, measuring about 9 inches (23cm) across the top, cover and leave to rise until at least doubled in size. This will take around 8 hours in the summer, but allow 9–10 hours in a cooler kitchen during the winter.

Carefully tip the dough out onto a floured surface and begin to stretch the outside edge into the middle – don't push too hard, you want to keep as much air in the dough as possible. Rotate the dough 90° and repeat. Continue in this way until you've gone around the dough a few times, then turn it over gently. Push a plastic bench scraper underneath, rotate the dough 90° and repeat several times. This action will tighten the top of the dough and smooth it off.

Put the dough in a floured banneton or in the middle of a long piece of parchment paper (which makes it easier to lift the dough into the pan). Leave to rest for a further 1–2 hours.

Heat your oven to 450°F and put a heavy-based ovenproof saucepan with a domed lid inside to heat up for 10 minutes.

If using a banneton to shape the dough, put a large sheet of parchment paper over the top of it and carefully invert the dough onto the paper.

Protecting your hands with oven mitts, bring the hot pan over to the dough. Using the parchment paper, carefully lift the dough into the hot pan and tuck it down around the sides. Cut off the excess paper.

Using a very sharp blade, cut a deep cross or hashtag in the top of the dough. Put the lid on the pan and put in the oven. Bake for 25 minutes, then remove the lid and bake for a further 30 minutes until well browned.

Lift your sourdough out of the pan and put on a wire rack to cool for 2 hours before eating. Delicious eaten freshly baked, the sourdough is also excellent toasted and makes a great base for bruschetta.

Hot Cross Buns

Makes about 12

I love hot cross buns and make them all year round, not just at Easter. The best part is glazing them fresh from the oven to give them their beautiful glossy shine. Adding fresh apple makes a big difference – go for a crisp variety, like Granny Smith or Pink Lady – or try clementine pieces for a bit of a change. The buns keep for 2 or 3 days, especially if you're going to toast them; they freeze well too.

———

Dough

4 cups (500g) bread flour, plus extra to dust

Scant 1 tsp (7g) fine salt

2 tbsp (30g) superfine sugar

1 large egg, beaten

3¾ tsp (10g) instant dried yeast

2 tbsp (30g) unsalted butter, softened

7 tbsp (100g) milk

½ cup plus 1 tbsp (140g) water

Filling

½ cup (80g) raisins

1 crisp apple, diced

⅓ cup (60g) diced candied peel, preferably a mixture of lemon and orange

Finely grated zest of 1 orange

1½ tsp ground cinnamon

Cross

1¼ cups (150g) all-purpose flour

½ cup (120g) water

Glaze

¾ cup (150g) superfine sugar

⅔ cup (150g) water

Finely grated zest of ½ lemon

Combine all of the dough ingredients in a large bowl and stir together for 30 seconds or so to form a dough that comes together in a ball (see page 90). Tip onto a lightly floured surface and knead well for 10 minutes (**1**). Alternatively, use a stand mixer fitted with the dough hook to mix and knead the dough, for 3 minutes on slow and 4 minutes on medium speed. Put the dough back in the bowl, cover with a large freezer bag and leave to rise for 1 hour.

For the filling, mix the ingredients together in another bowl. Add the filling to the dough and knead in until evenly distributed (**2**). Re-cover with a large freezer bag and leave to rise for a further hour.

Line a large baking sheet with parchment paper. Tip the dough onto a lightly floured surface and knock back to exclude the air. Divide into 12 equal pieces, each about ⅓ cup (75g) (**3**) and shape each piece into a ball (**4**). Put them in neat rows on the prepared baking sheet, leaving space in between to let the buns rise. Cover the baking sheet with a large freezer bag (**5**) and leave to proof for 1½ hours until at least doubled in size.

For the cross mixture, mix the flour and water together to form a paste and whisk well for a minute or two. Spoon into a pastry bag fitted with a fine plain tip. To make the glaze, in a saucepan over a medium heat, dissolve the sugar in the water, then take off the heat and let cool before adding the lemon zest.

Heat your oven to 400°F. Once your buns are proofed, pipe a horizontal line across the middle of each one, then turn the baking sheet 90° and repeat, crossing the first lines (**6**). You should now have a cross on every bun. Bake the hot cross buns for 15–20 minutes, or until a deep golden-brown color.

As you take the buns from the oven, brush the cooled glaze all over the tops (**7**), then repeat to give them a second coat. Transfer the buns to a wire rack to cool. Serve while still slightly warm if you can, or enjoy toasted with butter.

Steps illustrated overleaf

5

6

Iced Finger Buns

Makes 11

These take me back to being a kid when my father would bring iced doughnuts home from the bakery. They're made with the same dough as doughnuts but they're baked not fried. In the UK, you can get iced finger buns with all kinds of fillings and toppings, but I think you can't beat the fondant-dipped classic – split and filled with whipped cream and preserves, or simply buttered.

───

Dough

4 cups (500g) bread flour, plus extra to dust

1 tsp (8g) fine salt

¼ cup (50g) superfine sugar

3¾ tsp (10g) instant dried yeast

3 tbsp (50g) butter, cut into pieces and softened

7 tbsp (100g) tepid milk

½ cup (130g) water

1 large egg, beaten

Fondant icing

2 cups (200g) confectioners' sugar, sifted

Finely grated zest of 1 lemon

About ¼ cup (60ml) water

To serve

1 cup (250g) heavy cream

7 tbsp (100g) strawberry preserves, warmed and strained

To make the dough, mix the flour, salt, sugar and yeast in a large bowl. Add the butter and rub together for 30 seconds or so. Add the remaining ingredients and stir until you have a rough dough that comes together as a ball. Fold the dough into the middle, rotate the bowl 90° and repeat this for a few minutes until the dough is smooth. Tip out onto a lightly floured surface and knead well for 10 minutes. Alternatively, use a stand mixer fitted with the dough hook to mix and knead the dough, for 4 minutes on slow and 5 minutes on medium speed.

Return the dough to the bowl, cover with plastic wrap and leave to rise for 2 hours or until doubled in size.

Line two large baking sheets with parchment paper. Tip the dough out onto a lightly floured surface and fold it inwards repeatedly to knock out the air. Divide into 11 equal pieces, each about ⅓ cup (80g). Flatten each piece and roll up like a jelly roll. Flatten the edges and fold under, then gently roll again into a sausage shape, 4¾ inches (12cm) long. Put the rolls, seam side down, on the prepared baking sheets, leaving space in between to let the dough rise. Put each baking sheet in a roomy freezer bag and leave the buns to proof for 2 hours until at least doubled in size.

Heat your oven to 415°F. Bake the buns for 10–15 minutes until the tops and bases are golden brown. Leave to cool on the baking sheets.

For the fondant icing, mix the confectioners' sugar with the lemon zest and enough water to make a glossy icing with a thick, pourable consistency. Dip the top of each bun into the icing briefly then run your finger across the top of the bun to spread the icing evenly. Leave to set on a wire rack for 2 hours.

Whip the heavy cream until holding (not quite stiff) peaks and put in a pastry bag fitted with a ½-inch (1cm) star tip. Slice each bun through the middle, almost but not quite right through. Pipe a spiral of cream along the bottom half of each bun. Put the preserves into a paper pastry bag, snip off the very tip and pipe a line of preserves on top of the cream. Sandwich together gently and serve.

Orange Brioche

Makes 2 loaves

I used to make loads of brioche for breakfast when I worked at The Dorchester, Chester Grosvenor and Cliveden House hotels back in the nineties. This version is so light and fluffy and has a gorgeous aroma of orange. Toasted, it's absolute perfection, but be careful: because of the high sugar content, the brioche slices only need toasting for 10–20 seconds. Brioche toast is also great with pâté, and any leftovers make a fantastic bread pudding.

4 cups (500g) bread flour, plus extra to dust

scant 1 tsp (7g) fine salt

¼ cup (50g) superfine sugar

3¾ tsp (10g) instant dried yeast

5 large eggs

7 tbsp (100g) warm whole milk

Finely grated zest of 2 oranges

2 sticks plus 1 tbsp (250g) unsalted butter, softened, plus extra to grease

———

Put the flour, salt, sugar, yeast, eggs and warm milk into a stand mixer fitted with the dough hook. Mix on a slow speed for 2 minutes to combine the ingredients, then increase the speed to medium for 10 minutes to form a soft, elastic dough.

Add the orange zest and softened butter, in pieces, and continue to mix on medium speed for a further 5 minutes to loosen the dough and slowly begin to stretch it. It should now be shiny and soft to the touch.

Scrape the dough into a lidded 1½–2-quart plastic container, cover and put in the fridge overnight to rise slowly for at least 6 hours. During this time the dough will firm up and become easier to shape. The lengthy resting also allows the brioche to develop a beautiful fermented smell.

Grease two 1-pound (500g) loaf pans with butter. Tip the dough out onto a lightly floured surface and divide into 22 equal pieces, each about ¼ cup (50g). Shape these pieces into balls on the table or in your hands.

Put the dough balls in the prepared pans, starting with two balls side by side at one end of each pan, then one, then two side by side, continuing in this way until each pan is filled with two layers of balls.

Put each loaf pan in a roomy freezer bag and leave to proof at room temperature for 2–3 hours until the dough has risen to the rim of the pans.

Heat your oven to 400°F. Bake the brioche for 30 minutes or until a skewer inserted into the center comes out clean. Leave in the pans to cool for 5 minutes, then remove and put on a wire rack to cool. Serve while still warm or fully cooled.

English Muffins

Makes 4

These were very popular served with eggs Benedict when I worked at Cliveden House Hotel. They're also perfect for making your own version of a popular fast food breakfast sandwich! It's a simple dough but the secret to getting the muffins right is having your pan at the right temperature. Too hot and it'll burn the outside but the inside will be raw; too low and it will dry out.

2⅓ cups plus 1 tbsp (300g) **bread flour**, plus extra to dust

1 tsp (3g) **instant dried yeast**

1 tsp (8g) **fine salt**

1 tbsp (15g) **superfine sugar**

1 tbsp plus 1 tsp (20g) **unsalted butter**, diced and softened

1 large **egg**

Up to scant 1 cup (170–200g) **milk**

A little oil, for oiling

Semolina, to sprinkle

In a large bowl, combine the flour, yeast, salt and sugar. Add the butter, egg and ⅔ cup (150g) of the milk and turn the mixture round with your fingers to mix. Continue to add the remaining milk until all the flour is incorporated and you have a smooth dough; you may not need all of the milk. Tip the dough onto a lightly floured surface and knead for 8–10 minutes. Alternatively, use a stand mixer fitted with the dough hook to mix and knead the dough, for 3–4 minutes on slow and 4–5 minutes on medium speed.

Put the dough in a lightly oiled bowl, cover with plastic wrap and leave to rise for an hour or until doubled in size.

Line a large baking sheet with parchment paper. Tip the dough out onto a lightly floured surface and roll out to a ¾-inch (2cm) thickness. Using a 3½-inch (8½cm) biscuit cutter, stamp out 4 rounds.

Put the dough rounds on the prepared baking sheet and sprinkle the tops evenly with a little semolina. Put the baking sheet in a roomy freezer bag and leave to proof for about an hour or until risen slightly.

Heat a heavy-based frying pan, skillet or griddle over a low heat and wipe the surface of the pan with an oiled piece of paper towel. Cook the muffins in the pan, in batches, for 5–6 minutes on each side. Transfer to a wire rack and leave to cool completely.

To serve, slice the muffins in half and toast them, then spread with butter.

The Ultimate Focaccia

Makes 1 large focaccia

I'll often take one of these with me if I'm going to a dinner party – it always disappears very quickly! There's a lot of water in the dough which you need, as otherwise you can end up with a cakey texture. Focaccia is simple to make though, because it's in a pan, so there's only one way for it to go. Make sure you push the olives, tomatoes and onions right down into the indentations and use plenty of olive oil on the bottom and drizzled over the top. And don't over-bake this one; you want it to stay light and soft inside.

———

Dough

4 cups (500g) bread flour

1 tsp (8g) fine salt

3¾ tsp (10g) instant dried yeast

2 tbsp (30g) olive oil, plus extra for oiling

1½ cups (370g) water

Topping

½ cup (75g) pitted Kalamata black olives

1 small red onion

10 cherry or grape tomatoes

1 tbsp dried oregano

About ⅔ cup (135g) olive oil, to drizzle

Flaky sea salt

Put all of the dough ingredients into a large bowl and stir together to combine and form a dough (see page 90). Fold a corner of the dough into the middle and push firmly (**1**), then rotate the bowl 90° and repeat. Continue this folding and turning action for 2 minutes then tip the dough out onto a lightly oiled surface and knead for 10 minutes until soft and elastic. Alternatively, use a stand mixer fitted with the dough hook to mix and knead the dough, for 2 minutes on slow and 7 minutes on medium speed.

Put the dough back in the bowl, cover with a large freezer bag and leave to rise at room temperature for 2 hours until at least doubled in size.

Liberally oil the base of a large, shallow baking pan, about 9 x 13 inches (22½ x 32½cm). Tip the dough out onto a lightly oiled surface and stretch it to fit the dimensions of the prepared pan. Drizzle with lots of olive oil (**2**) and make firm indentations all over the surface with your fingers. Put the pan into a roomy freezer bag and leave to proof for 1½ hours.

Remove the pan from the freezer bag and put the olives evenly on the dough, pressing them firmly in place. Cut the onion into slim wedges and distribute these over the dough, pushing them in too. Cut the cherry tomatoes in half and press them evenly into the dough (**3**). Drizzle with more olive oil (**4**) and sprinkle with the dried oregano and a generous amount of flaky sea salt.

Heat your oven to 450°F. Bake the focaccia for 20 minutes or until golden brown. As you take the focaccia from the oven, drizzle more olive oil over the surface. Transfer to a wire rack and leave to cool.

Steps illustrated overleaf

3

4

Naan

The beauty of naan is that they are so quick to cook – you slap them in a hot pan and they puff up in just a couple of minutes. This is a very versatile dough and I've experimented with lots of different flavorings over the years – from mango chutney and curry powder to mushrooms, Stilton and walnut, and even Brie and grapes. I've given two of my favorite variations here: a garlic version and one made with raisins.

2 cups (250g) bread flour,
plus extra to dust

½ tsp (5g) fine salt

1 tsp (5g) baking powder

1¾ tsp (5g) instant dried yeast

2 tbsp (10g) honey

1 tbsp plus 1 tsp (20g) butter,
softened

½ cup (130g) plain yogurt

A little sunflower oil,
for oiling

Put the flour, salt, baking powder and yeast into a large bowl and stir briefly. Make a well in the middle and add the remaining ingredients. Mix together, using one hand, until you have a rough dough that comes together as a ball (see page 90). Fold the dough into the middle, rotate the bowl 90° and repeat this for 3–5 minutes until the dough is smooth. Alternatively, use a stand mixer fitted with the dough hook to mix and knead the dough, for 3–4 minutes on slow and 4–5 minutes on medium speed.

Cover the bowl with plastic wrap and leave to rest for 30 minutes. Tip the dough out onto a lightly floured surface and fold a corner into the middle then rotate the dough 90° and repeat this process for a minute or so. Return the dough to the bowl, re-cover and leave to rest for a further 2 hours.

Tip the dough out onto a lightly floured surface and fold it inwards repeatedly to knock out the air. Divide into 5 equal pieces. Shape each one into a ball then flatten out with your hand to an oval shape, about 8 inches (20cm) long and 4–6 inches (10–15cm) wide, using a rolling pin to help if necessary.

Heat a large frying pan or skillet over a medium-high heat and wipe the pan with a little oil. When hot, lay one dough oval in the pan and dry-fry for 1–2 minutes until speckled with brown patches underneath, then turn and repeat on the other side. Transfer to a plate and keep warm while you cook the rest in the same way, piling the naan on top of one another to keep them soft. Serve immediately.

Garlic naan In a saucepan, melt 7 tablespoons (100g) lightly salted butter with 3 chopped garlic cloves. Prepare the naan as above. Once cooked, brush the surface well with garlic butter, then remove from the pan and brush the other side.

Raisin naan Prepare the naan dough as above but after it has rested for 30 minutes and you've turned it out onto a lightly floured surface, scatter ⅔ cup (100g) raisins over the dough and fold, as above, to distribute evenly. Rest again for a further 2 hours then shape and cook as above.

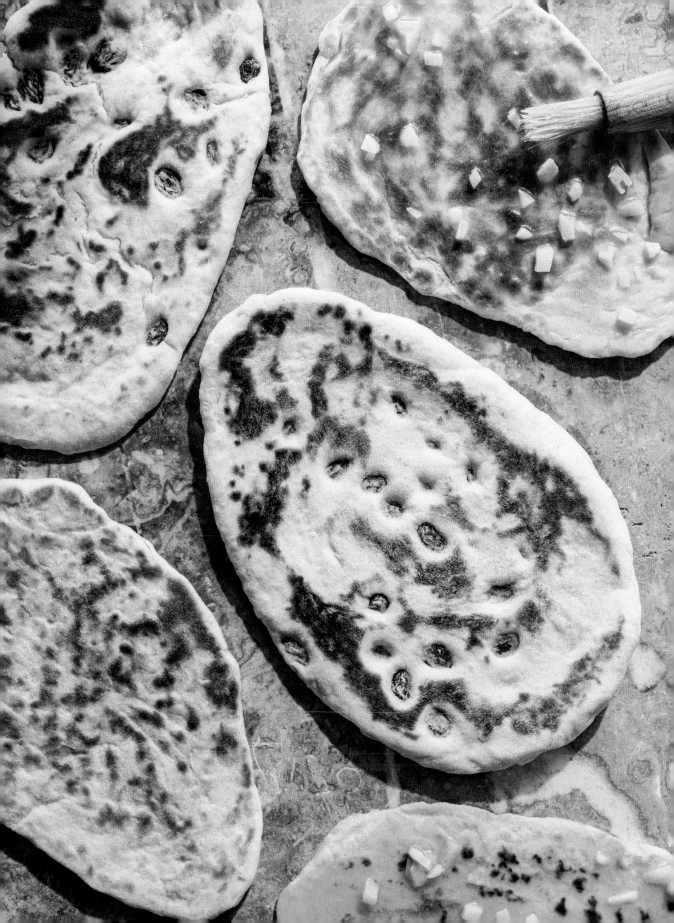

Lagana

Makes 1 large lagana

A Greek bread that is traditionally eaten at the start of Lent, lagana reminds me of my years living in Cyprus. It has a texture a little bit like focaccia but is lighter and uses less oil, and it's topped with sesame seeds. Here, I've used a mixture of white and black sesame seeds as well as caraway seeds for extra flavor. Mastic is a Greek spice that tastes slightly woody – like pine trees! Try to track some down if you can, for a truly authentic experience.

Dough

4 cups (500g) bread flour

Scant 1 tsp (7g) fine salt

3¾ tsp (10g) instant dried yeast

1 tsp (5g) ground mastic, optional

2 tbsp (30g) olive oil, plus extra for oiling

Up to 1⅓ cups (275–320g) water

Topping

⅔ cup (100g) black sesame seeds

4 tsp (15g) caraway seeds

1¼ cups (180g) white sesame seeds

Put the flour, salt, yeast, ground mastic (if using) and olive oil into a large bowl and pour in 1 cup (250g) of the water. Stir together for 1 minute to combine, then gradually incorporate enough of the remaining water to bring the mixture together to form a dough; you may not need all of it (see page 90). Fold a corner of the dough into the middle, rotate the bowl 90° and repeat. Continue this folding and turning action for 2 minutes then tip the dough out onto a lightly oiled surface and knead for 10 minutes until the dough is soft and elastic. Alternatively, use a stand mixer fitted with the dough hook to mix and knead the dough, for 2 minutes on slow and 7 minutes on medium speed.

Put the dough back in the bowl, cover with a large freezer bag and leave to rise at room temperature for 2–3 hours until doubled in size.

Have ready a large baking sheet. Tip the dough onto a lightly oiled surface and fold it inwards repeatedly to knock out the air.

Shape the dough into a ball and then roll into an oval shape, about 10 inches (25cm) in length. Make firm indentations all over the surface with your fingers.

Tip all of the seeds into a large shallow dish and pour a little boiling water over them, just enough to moisten but not cover them entirely. Give them a stir. Pick up the lagana and press the top and sides firmly into the seeds to coat well.

Put the seeded dough on the prepared baking sheet. Cover loosely with a freezer bag and leave to proof for 1 hour.

Heat your oven to 415°F. Bake the lagana for 25 minutes or until golden brown. Transfer to a wire rack to cool. Best eaten while still warm, with a Greek salad.

Pitas

Makes 4

My favorite food in the whole world is pork souvlaki, which I learned to love from living in Cyprus for six years. When I came back to the UK, I couldn't find the perfect pita bread to recreate it, so I developed this one. It's a basic dough, but the black sesame seeds give it a real taste of Cyprus. It's also a great recipe to make with the kids – they'll love watching the pita bread puff up in the oven like a balloon and then drop back down. The pitas freeze well too; just put them in the toaster to warm through.

———

Dough

2 cups (250g) bread flour, plus extra to dust

Scant 1 tsp (7g) fine salt

1 x ¼-oz (7g) envelope instant dried yeast

2 tbsp (30g) olive oil, plus extra for oiling

1 cup plus 2 tbsp (280g) water

Topping (optional)

⅓ cup (50g) black sesame seeds

To make the dough, in a large bowl, mix all the ingredients together with your hands until the mixture comes together and forms a dough (see page 90). Tip the dough onto a lightly oiled surface and knead well for 5–8 minutes until the dough is soft and elastic. Alternatively, use a stand mixer fitted with the dough hook to mix and knead the dough, for 2 minutes on slow and 5 minutes on medium speed.

Return the dough to the bowl, cover with a large freezer bag and leave to rise for 2 hours until doubled in size.

Heat your oven to 450°F and put a baking sheet or pizza stone on the middle shelf to heat up.

Tip the dough out onto a lightly floured surface and knock it back by folding the dough inwards over and over again for 5–10 minutes to knock out all the air.

Divide the dough into 4 equal pieces and shape into balls. Roll each ball into an oval, ⅛–¼ inch (3–5mm) thick. Sprinkle with the sesame seeds, if using, and press firmly to adhere.

You may need to cook the pitas in batches. Take the hot baking sheet or stone from the oven, dust it with flour and lay the pitas on it. Bake the pitas for 5–10 minutes, or until they just start to color.

Transfer to a plate, piling the pitas on top of one another and covering them with a clean cloth to keep them soft until they are cool.

Maneesh

Makes 5

I first ate maneesh on a trip to Morocco. It's a classic Middle Eastern flatbread, topped with za'atar, sesame seeds and olive oil. You can serve it with a meat dish or salads and use it to scoop up any sauce, but it has a delicious aromatic flavor on its own. It looks and tastes incredible but is very simple to make.

———

Dough

4 cups (500g) bread flour, plus extra to dust

1 tsp (8g) fine salt

1 tbsp (15g) superfine sugar

1 x ¼-oz (7g) envelope instant dried yeast

2 tbsp (30g) olive oil, plus extra for oiling

1¼ cups (290g) water

Za'atar Topping

2 tbsp (20g) sesame seeds

6 tbsp (12g) dried thyme

4 tbsp (8g) dried marjoram

A splash of olive oil

Put all of the dough ingredients into a large bowl and stir together briefly to combine (see page 90), then tip the dough out onto a lightly oiled surface and knead for 10 minutes until soft and elastic. Alternatively, use a stand mixer fitted with the dough hook to mix and knead the dough, for 2 minutes on slow and 7 minutes on medium speed.

Put the dough back in the bowl, cover with a large freezer bag and leave to rise at room temperature for 2 hours until doubled in size.

For the za'atar topping, mix the ingredients together in a small bowl. Heat your oven to 415°F. Have ready two or three large baking sheets.

Tip the dough out onto a lightly floured surface and fold it inwards repeatedly to knock out the air.

Divide the dough into 5 equal pieces. Shape each piece into a ball and roll out to an 8-inch (20cm) round.

Put the dough rounds on the baking sheets and brush the surface with a little water. Scatter the za'atar topping evenly on top of them. Bake for 15 minutes until golden brown. Transfer to a wire rack and leave to cool.

Tortillas

Makes 10

These are impressive, yet so easy. It's just a five-minute dough made from flour, salt, water and olive oil. My only tips are to use a heavy rolling pin if you have one, to roll them out thinly, and to cook them very quickly in a hot pan – give them no more than 90 seconds. They're great served with a Mexican feast and ideal for making burritos.

4 cups (500g) bread flour

1 tsp (8g) fine salt

1¼ cups (300g) water

A splash of olive oil, plus extra for oiling

In a large bowl, mix all the ingredients together with your hands until the mixture comes together and forms a dough. Tip out onto a lightly oiled surface and knead well for 5 minutes until smooth.

Put the dough back in the bowl, cover with a large freezer bag and leave to rest for 1 hour.

Divide the dough into about 10 equal-sized pieces and shape each into a ball. (Try not to use flour on the surface when shaping.) Roll each piece out thinly to a large round, the size of a large frying pan.

Heat a heavy-based frying pan or skillet over a medium-high heat and dry-fry each tortilla for 1½ minutes on each side; you should get little dark bubbles on the underside. Transfer to a plate.

Keep warm while you cook the rest of the tortillas in the same way, piling them on top of one another once they are cooked to keep them soft. Serve straight away.

Chapatis

Makes 5

These are traditionally cooked over flames, but we're making things easy by using a hot frying pan here. Although you'll achieve the best results by leaving the dough to proof for an hour, if you've forgotten to order chapatis with your Indian takeout, you can actually make these in under half an hour – leaving them to rest for just 5 or so minutes. When you cook them, they puff up like a ball and then you flip them over to cook on the other side. So simple.

1⅔ cups (200g) whole wheat flour

⅓ cup (50g) all-purpose flour

½ tsp fine salt

A splash of olive oil, plus extra for oiling

½ cup (120g) water

Put all the ingredients into a large bowl and stir together with a wooden spoon to form a rough dough. Tip out onto a lightly oiled surface and knead for a few minutes until smooth.

Put the dough back in the bowl, cover and leave to rest for 1 hour.

Divide the dough into 5 balls and roll each out to a circle, approximately 6 inches (15cm) in diameter.

Heat a heavy-based frying pan or skillet over a medium heat. When hot, add one of the dough rounds and dry-fry for 1½–2 minutes on each side until speckled with brown patches.

Transfer to a plate and keep warm while you cook the rest in the same way, piling the chapatis on top of one another once they are cooked to keep them soft. Serve immediately.

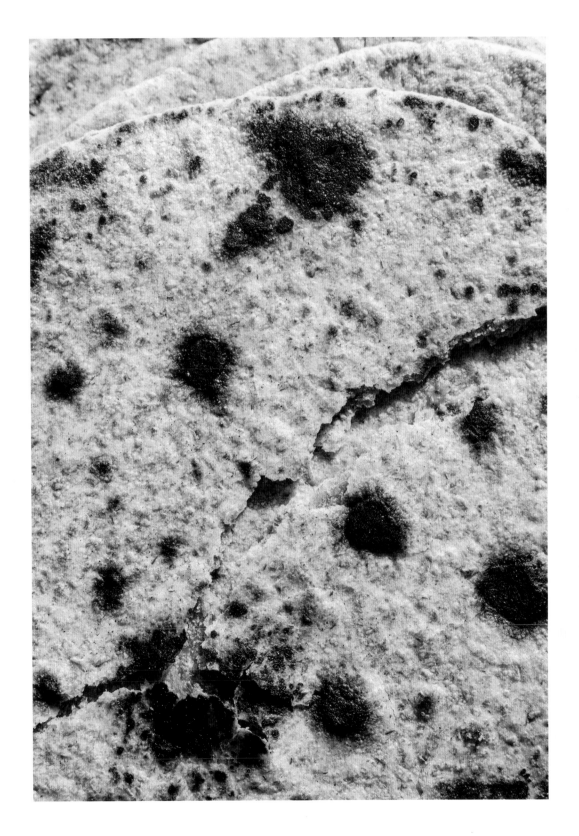

Olive Sticks
with Manchego

Makes 14–16

Once you start eating these, you won't be able to stop! They're so moreish. They're more like olives surrounded with a little bit of crispy bread than bread with olives in it. And the addition of Manchego cheese takes it all to the next level. Serve the crunchy sticks with dips, like baba ganoush, or as a canapé before a meal. You will need to use a stand mixer to mix and knead this dough as it is too wet and sticky to handle.

4 cups (500g) bread flour, plus extra to dust

Scant 1 tsp (7g) fine salt

3¾ tsp (10g) instant dried yeast

2 tbsp (30g) olive oil, plus extra for oiling

1½ cups (360g) water

3¼ cups (400g) pitted large green olives

6 oz (150g) Manchego, cut into small dice

To finish

1½ cups (150g) freshly grated Parmesan

Put the flour, salt, yeast, olive oil and 1¼ cups (300g) of the water into a stand mixer fitted with the dough hook and mix on a slow speed for 3 minutes to combine. Increase the speed to medium for 10 minutes, to form a firm dough. Continuing to mix, slowly add the remaining water over a couple of minutes, then mix for a further 4 minutes. Add the olives and diced cheese and mix the dough on a slow speed for another 5 minutes.

Scrape the dough into a well-oiled 2½-quart (2½-liter) plastic square container with a lid. Cover and leave the dough to rise for 2–3 hours until more than doubled in size.

Gently tip the dough out onto a well-floured surface and tap into a rectangle, about 16 x 12 inches (40 x 30cm), using a plastic bench scraper; the dough will be very loose. Dust the top of the dough generously with flour to prevent too much sticking.

Have ready several baking sheets. Cut a 1¾-inch (4cm) strip from the shorter side of the dough rectangle (for ease, I use a bench scraper to do this). Roll the strip lightly in flour, divide in half and put on a baking sheet, stretching each piece out until 8 inches (20cm) in length. Repeat to cut the rest of the sticks.

Once all the pieces have been cut and stretched on the baking sheets, put each sheet in a roomy freezer bag and leave to proof for 20 minutes.

Heat your oven to 425°F. Brush each dough stick lightly with water and sprinkle with the grated Parmesan. Bake for 15–20 minutes until golden. Transfer the olive sticks to a wire rack and leave to cool.

3

4

5

Pizzas
and
Doughnuts

If I were to choose my last meal on Earth, it would be very difficult not to include a good pizza and a doughnut. They are some of the best things to eat in the world. I don't know many people who don't like eating a pizza. With so much flexibility when it comes to the toppings, it's something everyone can enjoy.

I've become a bit obsessed with making pizzas over the last few years. I like the traditional Roman-style pizzas, which have a thin, crispy base, a strong color and a slightly soft middle that bends. It's a classic pizza. It's not a few centimeters thick – you wouldn't get that in Italy – and it's not a stuffed crust. I want my pizzas to be as close to an authentic pizza as possible.

The trick to a perfect crisp base is getting the oven as hot as you can. I have an outdoor pizza oven at home, which can reach temperatures higher than 575°F but you can still achieve something very similar in a domestic oven, and the recipes in this chapter provide instructions for both. Dry-frying the pizza base first is a simple way to get the base extra crispy and means it won't take as long to cook in the oven, so you won't risk overcooking your toppings. (See page 158 for how to do this.)

A pizza really is only as good as the quality of its ingredients so use the best you can find. I've perfected my dough (page 158) and I blitz canned San Marzano tomatoes for the sauce. They're some of the tastiest tomatoes in the world and you don't need to add anything else to them. When you're thinking about toppings, less is more, especially when it comes to cheese – don't overload it. I think you can't beat the traditional combinations: Margherita, garlic and mushroom, quattro formaggi, and prosciutto and mushroom (pages 160, 164, 166 and 170 respectively). Even if I'm blowing my own horn, I have to say my pizzas are very good! You can also freeze the pizza dough, so you have some ready to go.

After your pizza, what could be better than a doughnut? Although they're fried not baked, they are so incredible, I had to include them in this book. I love them with a cup of coffee late morning or as a dessert. My absolute favorite is the lemon doughnut on page 178 – it reminds me of being a kid – but for something really decadent I'd suggest making the chocolate doughnuts on page 180. Or, for a twist on the theme, try the chouxnuts on page 182, which are made from deep-fried choux pastry filled with a lemony cream and topped with glacé icing. It's the absolute best way to finish an indulgent meal.

Pizza Dough

Makes 4 bases

It's really easy to make your own pizza dough, especially if you use a stand mixer to mix and knead the dough. The secret to a good pizza is to roll the dough out as thinly as possible and to cook your pizzas in a very hot oven. If you haven't got an outdoor pizza oven, get your oven as hot as you can; I also recommend dry-frying the pizza bases before topping and baking them to help give you a crisper base, as described below.

———

4 cups (500g) bread flour

¼ cup (60g) sourdough starter (see page 121)

Scant 1 tsp (7g) fine salt

1¾ tsp (5g) instant dried yeast

1 tbsp plus 1 tsp (20g) superfine sugar

2 tbsp (30g) olive oil, plus extra for oiling

1 cup plus 2 tbsp (270g) water

Put all the ingredients into a large bowl and mix together, using one hand or a wooden spoon, to combine the mixture until you have a soft dough that comes together as a ball. Tip the dough out onto a lightly oiled surface and knead well for 10 minutes until smooth and elastic. Alternatively, use a stand mixer fitted with the dough hook to mix and knead the dough, for 2 minutes on a slow speed and 7 minutes on medium.

Put the dough back into the bowl, cover with a large freezer bag and leave to rise for at least 2 hours, ideally 3–4 hours if you have time.

Tip your risen pizza dough out onto a lightly floured surface and divide into four equal pieces, each about ¾ cup (200g) . Flatten down each piece then fold it over and put in a cage formed by your cupped hand on the work surface. Move your hand in a circular motion to roll each ball lightly but firmly into a smooth, taut ball. Leave the balls to rest on the floured surface covered with a roomy freezer bag, to prevent them from drying and cracking, for about 30 minutes.

Roll out and stretch each ball of dough on a lightly floured surface to a thin circle, 10–12 inches (25–30cm) in diameter.

If you are using an outdoor pizza oven, you can top the bases now with your chosen ingredients and bake them in the intense heat for 1–1½ minutes.

To dry-fry pizza bases If you are using the oven in your home kitchen, I suggest dry-frying the bases before topping and baking them. Heat up a large frying pan or skillet over a high heat, then put one of the dough rounds in the pan and cook for 1 minute on each side so it takes on some color. Transfer to a plate and repeat to dry-fry the other pizza bases. Pile them on top of one another to keep them soft as you cook the rest. The dry-fried bases can be frozen, if required.

Pizza Margherita

Makes 4

There's nowhere to hide with a Margherita pizza, so you have to get every element just right. Using good-quality tinned San Marzano tomatoes is key here. A good creamy buffalo mozzarella and a few basil leaves are all you need to finish it off. Simple, but absolute perfection.

1 quantity pizza dough, shaped into 4 balls and ready to roll out (see page 158)

Topping

1 x 14-oz (400g) can whole peeled San Marzano tomatoes, drained

⅓ cup (30g) freshly grated Parmesan

14 oz (375g) buffalo mozzarella

A handful of basil leaves, roughly torn

Extra virgin olive oil, to drizzle

———

For the topping, using a blender or food processor, blitz the canned tomatoes until smooth.

If you are using a standard domestic oven to cook your pizzas, heat to its highest setting.

Roll out each ball of dough to a thin round (**1**). If using a domestic oven, dry-fry as described on page 158.

Put a small ladleful of tomato pulp in the middle of each pizza base (dry-fried if cooking in a standard oven, uncooked if using a pizza oven, see below) and spread out to about 1 inch (2–3cm) from the edge (**2**). Sprinkle with the grated Parmesan, then break off little pieces of mozzarella and scatter all over the tomatoes (**3**).

Bake each pizza on a baking sheet in the hot oven for 5–7 minutes until the topping is melted and golden and the pizza crust is crisp. Scatter the basil over the pizzas and drizzle with extra virgin olive oil. Serve at once.

Outdoor pizza oven Heat up your pizza oven. Roll out your pizza bases to 10–12 inches (25–30cm, see page 158). Prepare the topping (as above) and distribute over the uncooked bases. Bake in the hot oven for 1 minute–1 minute 20 seconds.

Steps illustrated overleaf

3

Garlic and Mushroom Pizza

Makes 4

This pizza is all about the garlic butter. Simply chop up the garlic, cook it in the melted butter to let the flavor infuse and leave it to cool. When you take your pizza out of the oven, brush it all over with the garlicky butter. I promise it will blow your mind and be the best garlic bread you'll ever eat!

1 quantity pizza dough, shaped into 4 balls and ready to roll out (see page 158)

Topping

1 stick plus 5 tbsp (200g) butter

4 garlic cloves, chopped

2 tbsp olive oil

2½ cups (200g) sliced cremini mushrooms

Scant ½ cup (40g) freshly grated Parmesan

14 oz (375g) buffalo mozzarella

To prepare the topping, in a small saucepan over a low heat, slowly melt the butter. Add the chopped garlic and simmer for 3 minutes.

Heat the olive oil in a frying pan, add the mushrooms and sauté for a few minutes to soften until starting to color, then tip into a strainer to drain off the excess liquor.

If you are using a standard domestic oven to cook your pizzas, heat to its highest setting.

Roll out each ball of dough to a thin round. If using a domestic oven, dry-fry as described on page 158.

Sprinkle each pizza base (dry-fried if cooking in a standard oven, uncooked if using a pizza oven, see below) with the grated Parmesan. Break off little pieces of mozzarella and scatter over the surface of the pizza, leaving a 1-inch (2–3cm) border around the edge. Distribute the sautéed mushrooms over the top.

Bake each pizza on a baking sheet in the hot oven for 5–7 minutes until the cheese is melted and golden and the pizza crust is crisp. As you take the pizzas from the oven, brush all over with the melted garlicky butter and serve immediately.

Outdoor pizza oven Heat up your pizza oven. Roll out your pizza bases to 10–12 inches (25–30cm, see page 158). Prepare the topping (as above) and distribute over the uncooked bases. Bake in the hot oven for 1 minute–1 minute 20 seconds. Brush the pizzas with the garlicky butter as you take them from the oven. Serve at once.

Quattro Formaggi Pizza

Makes 4

I've used a classic combination of Parmesan, mozzarella, Cheddar and dolcelatte in this decadent four-cheese pizza, but feel free to play around with different types of cheeses. The only rule is less is more. If you use too much cheese, it can end up rubbery. You can use five or six varieties if you like – but only a little of each. Then, as you get used to how the different cheeses melt, you can adjust the quantities.

1 quantity pizza dough, shaped into 4 balls and ready to roll out (see page 158)

Topping

1 x 14-oz (400g) can whole peeled San Marzano tomatoes, drained

1 cup (100g) freshly grated Parmesan

14 oz (375g) buffalo mozzarella

6 oz (150g) dolcelatte

1½ cups (150g) grated Cheddar or Gruyère

For the topping, using a blender or food processor, blitz the canned tomatoes until smooth.

If you are using a standard domestic oven to cook your pizzas, heat to its highest setting.

Roll out each ball of dough to a thin round. If using a domestic oven, dry-fry as described on page 158.

Put a small ladleful of tomato pulp in the middle of each pizza base (dry-fried if cooking in a standard oven, uncooked if using a pizza oven, see below) and spread out to about 1 inch (2–3cm) from the edge. Sprinkle with the grated Parmesan. Now rip small pieces of the mozzarella and scatter over the surface. Do the same with the dolcelatte. Sprinkle the grated Cheddar or Gruyère over the top.

Bake each pizza on a baking sheet in the hot oven for 5–7 minutes until the cheese is melted and golden and the pizza crust is crisp. Serve immediately.

Outdoor pizza oven Heat up your pizza oven. Roll out your pizza bases to 10–12 inches (25–30cm, see page 158). Prepare the topping (as above) and distribute over the uncooked bases. Bake in the hot oven for 1 minute–1 minute 20 seconds.

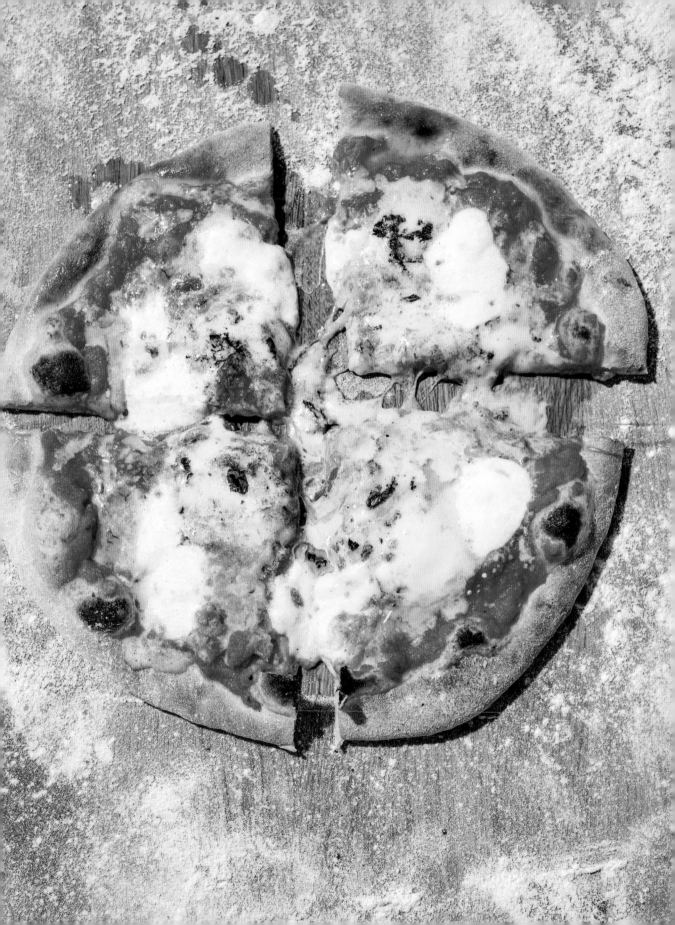

Prosciutto and Mushroom Pizza

Makes 4

If I'm going to an Italian pizzeria, this is the pizza I always order. It's got a bit of everything – gorgeous tomatoes, salty chewy ham, mushrooms and creamy, melted cheese. You can use cooked ham from a deli if you prefer, but I love the layer of thinly sliced prosciutto on top. To make it even more special, I sometimes swirl a little spiral of heavy cream around the middle of the pizza just before it goes in the oven.

1 quantity pizza dough, shaped into 4 balls and ready to roll out (see page 158)

Topping

Generous ½ x 14-oz can (250g) whole peeled San Marzano tomatoes, drained

2 tbsp olive oil

Heaping 3 cups (250g) sliced cremini mushrooms

⅓ cup (30g) freshly grated Parmesan

14 oz (375g) buffalo mozzarella

8 slices of prosciutto

———

For the topping, using a blender or food processor, blitz the tomatoes until smooth.

Heat the olive oil in a frying pan, add the sliced mushrooms and sauté for a few minutes to soften, until starting to color, then tip into a strainer to drain off the excess liquor.

If you are using a standard domestic oven to cook your pizzas, heat to its highest setting.

Roll out each piece to a thin round. If using a domestic oven, dry-fry as described on page 158.

Put a small ladleful of tomato pulp in the middle of each pizza base (dry-fried if cooking in a standard oven, uncooked if using a pizza oven, see below) and spread out to about 1 inch (2–3cm) from the edge. Sprinkle the grated Parmesan over the tomato. Now rip small pieces of the mozzarella and scatter over the surface. Top with the sautéed mushrooms.

Bake each pizza on a baking sheet in the hot oven for 5–7 minutes until the cheese is melted and golden and the pizza crust is crisp. As you take the pizzas from the oven, lay the slices of prosciutto across them. Serve immediately.

Outdoor pizza oven Heat up your pizza oven. Roll out your pizza bases to 10–12 inches (25–30cm, see page 158). Prepare the topping (as above) and distribute over the uncooked bases. Bake in the hot oven for 1 minute–1 minute 20 seconds. Top the pizzas with the prosciutto slices and serve at once.

Creamed Jelly Doughnuts

Makes 12

A cream-filled doughnut after school was always such a treat for me. You can get so many different flavors now, but I still don't think you can beat this British classic. The dough is enriched with sugar, butter and egg, making it beautifully sweet and light. Once fried, the warm doughnuts are rolled in sugar, then filled with whipped cream and jelly. Fantastic.

_____

Dough

4 cups (500g) bread flour, plus extra to dust

1 tsp (8g) fine salt

¼ cup (40g) superfine sugar

2 tbsp (30g) butter, cut into small pieces, softened

1 large egg

4½ tsp (12g) instant dried yeast

7 tbsp (100g) milk

½ cup plus 1 tbsp (140g) water

To cook

Sunflower oil, for deep-frying

Coating and filling

¾ cup (150g) superfine sugar

Scant 1 cup (200g) heavy cream

7 tbsp (100g) seedless raspberry jelly

Put all the ingredients for the dough into a large bowl and stir for 1 minute, using one hand or a wooden spoon, until the mixture comes together as a rough dough. Tip out onto a lightly floured surface and knead well for 10 minutes until silky and smooth. Return the dough to the bowl, cover with a large freezer bag and leave for 2 hours until well risen.

Line two large baking sheets with parchment paper. Tip the dough out onto a lightly floured surface and divide into 12 equal pieces, each about ⅓ cup (75g). Flatten down each piece then fold it over (**1**). Put a ball in a cage formed by your cupped hand on the work surface and move your hand in a circular motion to roll it lightly but firmly (**2**) into a smooth, taut ball; don't use flour on the surface as the dough will slide – you want it to grip. Repeat to shape the rest. Put the dough balls on the prepared baking sheets, cover each baking sheet with a large freezer bag and leave to proof for 1 hour until roughly doubled in size (**3**).

Heat the oil in a deep fryer or other deep, heavy saucepan (it should be no more than one-third full) over a medium heat to 350°F (check with a candy thermometer). Deep fry the dough balls, 2 or 3 at a time, in the hot oil – they should start to take on color within a minute. Fry, without moving, for 3 minutes, then turn over with a spoon, and deep fry for a further 2–3 minutes until golden brown all over.

Spread the sugar out on a baking sheet. Remove the doughnuts from the pan, using a slotted spoon, and drain on paper towels. Immediately put the doughnuts on the sheet, sprinkle them with sugar (**4**) and turn to coat all over (**5**). Put on a wire rack. Once all the doughnuts are fried and coated, leave to cool for 2 hours.

Whip the cream until holding (almost stiff) peaks and put into a pastry bag fitted with a ½-inch (1cm) star tip. Slice each doughnut vertically through the middle, about two-thirds of the way down. Pipe in a spiral of cream (**6**). Put the jelly into a paper pastry bag, snip off the very tip and pipe a zigzag of jelly on top of the cream.

Steps illustrated overleaf

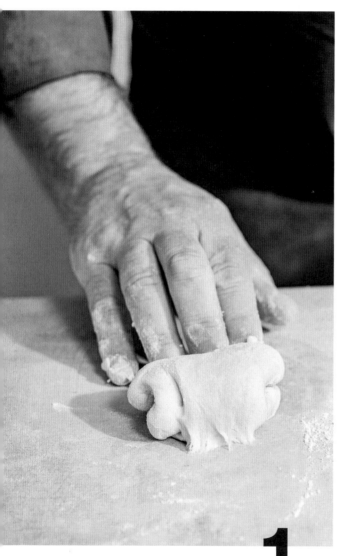

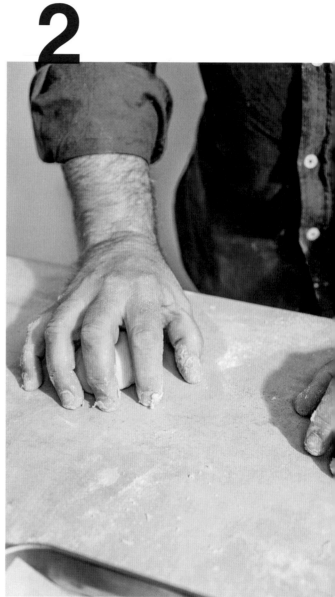

5

6

Lemon Doughnuts

Makes 12

When you bite into these doughnuts it's a whole feast of lemon. The water icing on top is made with lemon zest and is slightly crunchy, which contrasts beautifully with the fluffy doughnut dough and rich lemon curd filling. The only problem with these is it's very difficult to have just one...

———

Dough

4 cups (500g) bread flour, plus extra to dust

1 tsp (8g) fine salt

¼ cup (40g) superfine sugar

2 tbsp (30g) butter

1 large egg

4½ tsp (12g) instant dried yeast

7 tbsp (100g) milk

½ cup plus 1 tbsp (140g) water

To cook

Sunflower oil, for deep-frying

Lemon curd filling

Finely grated zest and juice of 4 lemons

Scant 1 cup (190g) superfine sugar

7 tbsp (100g) unsalted butter

3 large eggs

1 extra egg yolk

Lemon icing

1½ cups (150g) confectioners' sugar, sifted

Finely grated zest of 1 lemon

3 tbsp (40g) water

Put all the ingredients for the dough into a large bowl and stir for 1 minute, using one hand or a wooden spoon, until the mixture comes together as a rough dough. Tip out onto a lightly floured surface and knead well for 10 minutes until silky and smooth. Return the dough to the bowl, cover with a large freezer bag and leave for 2 hours until well risen.

Line two large baking sheets with parchment paper. Tip the dough out onto a floured surface and divide into 12 equal pieces, each about ⅓ cup (75g). Flatten each piece then fold it over and shape into balls (as for creamed jelly doughnuts, page 173). Put them on the prepared baking sheets, cover each sheet with a large freezer bag to prevent the dough drying out and leave to proof for 1 hour.

Heat the oil in a deep fryer or other deep, heavy saucepan (it should be no more than one-third full) to 350°F (check with a candy thermometer). Deep fry the dough balls, 2 or 3 at a time, in the hot oil – they should start to take on color within a minute. Fry, without moving, for 3 minutes, then turn over with a spoon, and deep fry for a further 2–3 minutes until golden brown all over.

Remove the doughnuts from the pan, using a slotted spoon, drain on paper towels then put on a wire rack. Leave to cool for 2 hours.

For the filling, put the lemon zest and juice, sugar and butter into a heatproof bowl over a saucepan of simmering water and stir until the butter is melted then take off the heat. In a separate bowl, beat the eggs with the extra yolk then whisk into the lemon mixture. Put back over the simmering water and stir well for 10–15 minutes until thickened. Pass the lemon curd through a strainer into a clean bowl. Leave to cool then spoon into a pastry bag fitted with a ¼-inch (5mm) plain tip.

For the lemon icing, in a medium bowl, mix the confectioners' sugar with the lemon zest and water to make a thin, glossy icing.

Using a sharp knife, make slits in the side of each doughnut and pipe in the lemon curd filling. Dip the doughnuts into the thin lemon icing to coat all over. Put on a wire rack and leave until the icing sets before serving.

Chocolate Doughnuts

Makes 12

Rich and delicious, these are seriously indulgent. Filled with a bittersweet chocolate cream and drizzled with melted white chocolate, they're irresistible, so if you're trying to lose some weight, look away now! Make a batch and share them – they're a chocolate-lover's dream.

―――――

Dough

4 cups (500g) bread flour, plus extra to dust

1 tsp (8g) fine salt

¼ cup (40g) superfine sugar

2 tbsp (30g) butter

1 large egg

4½ tsp (12g) instant dried yeast

7 tbsp (100g) milk

½ cup plus 1 tbsp (140g) water

To cook

Sunflower oil, for deep-frying

Filling and topping

¾ cup (150g) superfine sugar, to coat

1¼ cups (300g) heavy cream

7 oz (200g) bittersweet chocolate, in small pieces

7 oz (200g) white chocolate, in small pieces

Put all the ingredients for the dough into a large bowl and stir for 1 minute, using one hand or a wooden spoon, until the mixture comes together as a rough dough. Tip out onto a lightly floured surface and knead well for 10 minutes until silky and smooth. Return the dough to the bowl, cover with a large freezer bag and leave for 2 hours until well risen.

Line two large baking sheets with parchment paper. Tip the dough out onto a lightly floured surface and divide into 12 equal pieces, each about ⅓ cup (75g). Flatten down each piece then fold it over and shape into balls (as for creamed jelly doughnuts, page 173).

Put the dough balls on the prepared baking sheets, cover each sheet with a large freezer bag to prevent the dough drying out and leave to proof for 1 hour.

Heat the oil in a deep fryer or other deep, heavy pan (it should be no more than one-third full) to 350°F (check with a candy thermometer). Deep fry the dough balls, 2 or 3 at a time, in the hot oil – they should start to color within a minute. Fry, without moving, for 3 minutes, then turn using a spoon, and deep fry for a further 2–3 minutes until golden brown all over.

Spread the superfine sugar out on a large plate. Remove the doughnuts from the pan, using a slotted spoon, and drain on paper towels. Immediately put the doughnuts in the superfine sugar and turn to coat all over, then put on a wire rack. Once all the doughnuts are fried and coated, leave to cool for 2 hours.

For the filling, gently heat the cream in a saucepan then take off the heat, add the bittersweet chocolate and stir until fully melted. Leave to cool and thicken slightly. Make slits in the side of each doughnut. Put the cooled chocolate into a pastry bag fitted with a ¼-inch (5mm) plain tip and pipe into the slits in each doughnut.

Melt the white chocolate in a heatproof bowl over a saucepan of simmering water, making sure the base of the bowl is not touching the water. Stir until smooth then transfer to a paper pastry bag and snip off the very tip. Pipe lines of white chocolate all over the top of the doughnuts. Leave to set before serving.

Chouxnuts

Makes 8

A hybrid between choux pastry and a doughnut, these are deep-fried like a doughnut then filled with lemon curd and whipped cream and glazed with a lemony icing. A perfect combination of crisp pastry and tangy citrus flavors.

––––––

Choux pastry

⅔ cup (150g) water

4 tbsp (60g) butter

½ cup (60g) all-purpose flour

½ cup (60g) bread flour

3 large eggs

To cook

Sunflower oil, for deep-frying

Lemon curd filling

Finely grated zest and juice of 4 lemons

Scant 1 cup (190g) superfine sugar

7 tbsp (100g) butter, at room temperature, in pieces

3 large eggs

1 extra egg yolk

7 tbsp (100g) heavy cream, whipped

Lemon icing

1 cup (100g) confectioners' sugar, sifted

Finely grated zest of 1 lemon

About 2 tbsp (25g) water

First, make the lemon curd filling. Put the lemon zest and juice, sugar and butter into a heavy-based saucepan over a low heat and stir until the butter is fully melted then take off the heat. In a separate bowl, beat together the eggs and extra yolk then whisk into the lemon mixture. Put the pan back over a low heat and stir well for 10–15 minutes until thickened. Pass the lemon curd through a strainer into a clean bowl and let cool, before folding in the whipped cream.

To make the choux pastry, put the water and butter into a medium saucepan over a medium heat to melt the butter. Once the butter is melted, turn up the heat and bring to a boil, then take off the heat. Immediately add both flours and beat well to incorporate into the liquid. Continue to beat until the mixture forms a ball that pulls away from the side of the pan. Leave to cool slightly, for 5 minutes.

Transfer the mixture to a stand mixer fitted with the paddle beater. With the mixer on a low speed, slowly add the beaten eggs. Once all the egg has been incorporated, increase the speed to medium and beat until glossy and thick. The mixture should just about hold on the end of a spoon and feel silky.

Cut eight 5-inch (12cm) squares of parchment paper. Put the choux pastry into a pastry bag fitted with a ½-inch (1cm) star tip and pipe a ring, 4 inches (10cm) in diameter, on each paper square.

Heat the oil in a deep fryer or other deep, heavy pan over a medium heat to 350°F (check with a candy thermometer). You will need to deep fry your choux rings, 2 or 3 at a time: carefully lower into the oil, paper uppermost, then remove the paper with tongs. Deep fry the rings for 3–4 minutes. Drain and put on a wire rack. Cut a small hole in the side of each ring to let steam out and leave to cool.

Once cooled, make the hole in the side of each ring larger so you can insert a small piping tip. Put the lemon curd filling into a pastry bag fitted with a ¼-inch (5mm) plain tip and pipe into the choux rings to fill, until you meet resistance.

For the lemon icing, mix the confectioners' sugar with the lemon zest and enough water to make a glossy icing with a thick, pourable consistency. Brush over the top of each chouxnut to coat and leave to set before serving. Enjoy!

4

5

6

Pastry and Pies

Whether you're making a pie, a tart or a hand pie, the type of pastry you choose will make all the difference to your final bake. You can use shortcrust, puff, cheat's puff, rough puff or hot water crust; you can enrich the dough with eggs or milk; you can sweeten it with sugar, or add a little acidity with cream cheese; use all butter or a combination of lard, shortening and butter. They'll each bring their unique qualities but, ultimately, it's up to you to decide which pastry to use.

Traditionally, pigs in blankets are made with shortcrust pastry, but I like the buttery flakiness that you get from rough puff, so that's what I use in my pigs in blankets on page 202 and ultimate sausage roll on page 208. It also makes them more robust, which means they can hold more filling – always a good thing! But, of course, you can use shortcrust if you prefer. That's the beauty of baking: you can make it your own.

Although I know everyone will have their own views on this, I think a pie should really have a pastry base and a pastry lid. There are exceptions to this rule, of course – even a few that break the mold in this chapter, like the individual fish pot pies on page 190 – but mostly I think a pie needs to be enclosed, or *en croûte* as the French would say.

Hot water crust pastry is a fantastic medieval recipe for enclosed pies. I use it in my hand-raised Sunday lunch pie on page 214. It's made with lard, which helps it stay waterproof so it's particularly good for game and pork pies as it stops the meat juices leaking out. It was popular in Tudor times because Henry VIII loved his pies! In those days, everything was thrown in with a little bit of gravy and covered in pastry. That's essentially where the classic British steak and mushroom pie came from too (page 196).

As for sweet pies, they immediately feel cozy and comforting. Almost anywhere in the world you'll be able to find a pastry or pie filled with a local speciality, sweetened and maybe gently spiced. We had apple trees in our garden when I was growing up and now I have some in mine, too. Served with a big pitcher of crème anglaise, the apple pie recipe on page 218 brings back so many warm memories of home. Pecan pie, on the other hand, is something I was introduced to in America; made with molasses and golden syrup, it is sweet, crunchy and sticky, and has become an international classic for good reason. I urge you to give it a go – you'll find the recipe on page 231.

Pastry is such an amazingly versatile and flexible ingredient. Once you've got the hang of making it – and practice really does make perfect with pastry – you can simply choose a pastry and decide how you're going to fill it to start creating your own classics.

Pastry particulars

The role of gluten

To know what each pastry will bring to your bake, and therefore which one to choose, it's important to understand the role of gluten in flour. Gluten is the protein in flour that gives a dough its structure; you want to really work and develop the gluten in bread to allow it to rise beautifully, but you don't want to do this when it comes to pastry. You want a lighter touch. Shortcrust pastry should be handled only briefly, just bringing the dough together and not overworking it, so it stays light and crumbly. When it comes to the laminated doughs used for croissants and Danish pastries (pages 234 and 242), you do want that bit of extra elasticity, which is why I use a bread flour and knead the dough. Bread flour has a higher gluten content, and this helps to create the layers you want in the finished pastry.

Soggy bottom

'Soggy bottom' has practically become part of the English language now! When it comes to that dreaded soggy bottom, there is really only one trick to learn: blind baking the pie crust first to draw out the moisture. It involves lining your chilled pastry, once it is in its pan, with parchment paper and baking beans, and then baking for 12–15 minutes until it's just starting to color. You then remove the paper and beans and return the pie crust to the oven for 5 minutes or so to dry out the base. This will create a hardened base to which you can add your filling. It also means the pastry won't rise up any further when you cook it again. At this point you can trim the edges to create a neat, professional finish. You can also brush a little beaten egg onto your pastry base and put it back into the oven for a couple of minutes to create a seal between the pastry and the filling.

Chill out

If the recipe asks you to chill your pastry, make sure you do. This is so important, especially when it comes to laminated doughs. Don't think you can skip or rush this step. Chilling the pastry in the fridge lets the butter (or other fats) firm up, which makes it easier to roll. It also relaxes the pastry so it's less likely to shrink in the oven. In laminated doughs, if you don't properly chill the pastry at each stage, it won't have those light layers of pastry you're after in your final bake. Most of the recipes in this chapter require at least 30 minutes in the fridge. It's possible to speed up the chilling time, by freezing instead, but I'd suggest chilling the pastry in the fridge until you feel confident working with it.

Individual Fish Pot Pies

Makes 4

Delicate fish and shrimp cook perfectly in a velvety sauce beneath a blanket of buttery, flaky puff pastry. When you make a pie, you're essentially sealing everything in and cooking and steaming the filling in its own juices. Fish lends itself well to this gentle style of cooking as it helps keep it lovely and moist.

———

Puff pastry

¾ cup plus 1 tbsp (100g) bread flour

¾ cup plus 1 tbsp (100g) all-purpose flour, plus extra to dust

A pinch of fine salt

5–7 tbsp (75–100g) cold water

1 stick plus 3 tbsp (165g) cold unsalted butter

1 large egg, beaten, to glaze

Filling

2½ cups (600g) whole milk

1 bay leaf

1½ lbs (600g) mixed sustainable, firm white fish (such as cod or pollack) and salmon, skinless and boneless

3 tbsp (40g) butter, plus extra to grease the pie dishes

2½ tbsp (30g) all-purpose flour

Juice of ½ lemon

1 tsp English mustard

1 tbsp chopped parsley

4 oz (100g) large raw shrimp, shell off and deveined

Sea salt and black pepper

To make the puff pastry, combine the flours and salt in a large bowl. Mix in enough water to form a reasonably tight but still kneadable dough. Turn out onto a lightly floured surface and knead for 5–10 minutes until smooth. Form the dough into a rough rectangle, wrap in plastic wrap and rest in the fridge for at least an hour.

Using a rolling pin, bash the butter on a floured surface to flatten to a rectangle, 8 inches (20cm) long and just less than 4¾ inches (12cm) wide. Wrap in plastic wrap and chill in the fridge for 30 minutes.

Roll out the chilled dough to a rectangle, 4¾ x 12 inches (12 x 30cm). Lay the chilled butter on the dough so it covers the bottom two-thirds. Make sure it's positioned neatly and comes almost to the edges of the dough.

Lift the exposed dough at the top and fold down over half of the butter. Fold the butter-covered bottom half of the dough up over the top. You will now have a sandwich of two layers of butter and three of dough. Press or pinch the edges together to seal. Wrap in plastic wrap and chill in the fridge for an hour.

Remove the dough and turn it 90° so you have a short end towards you, then roll it into a long rectangle. Fold the top quarter down and the bottom quarter up so they meet in the middle. Then fold the dough in half along the center line and press or pinch the edges together to seal. Re-wrap and chill for 1 hour.

Remove the dough from the fridge, turn it 90° so a short end is facing you and roll it into a long rectangle. Fold one-third down, then fold the bottom third up over the top. Press or pinch the edges to seal. Wrap the pastry and chill for 1 hour.

Repeat this last stage of rolling, folding and chilling three more times and then chill the well-wrapped pastry dough overnight (or for at least 6 hours).

Continued overleaf

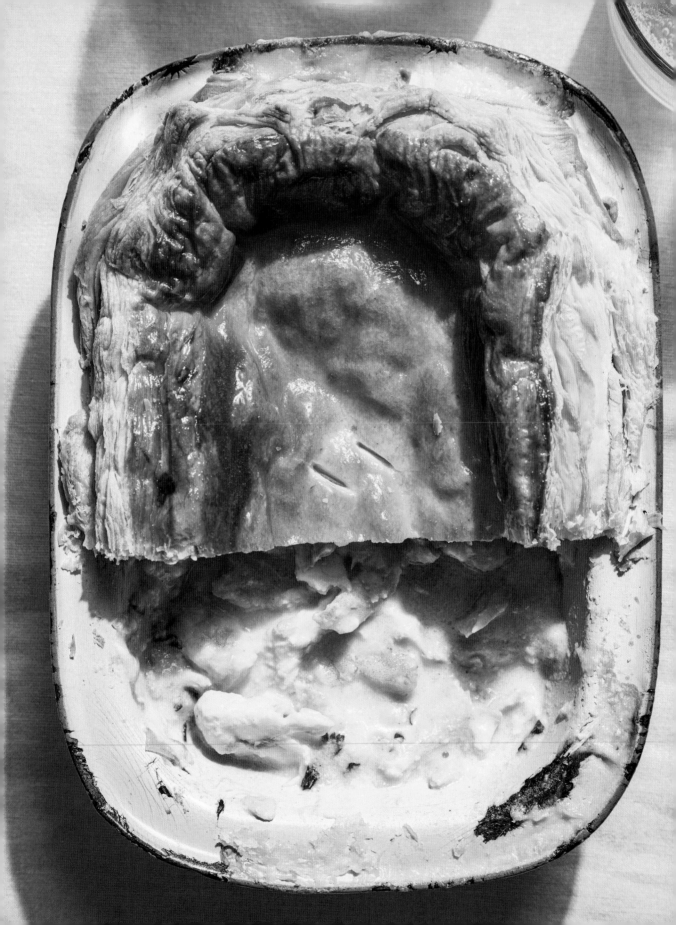

Heat your oven to 350°F. Lightly butter 4 individual pie dishes.

For the filling, in a deep-sided frying pan, bring the milk to a boil with the bay leaf added over a medium heat. Add the fish, lower the heat and poach gently for 4–6 minutes to partially cook. Lift out the fish onto a plate and let cool slightly. When cool enough to handle, flake the fish into bite-sized pieces and check for any stray bones. Strain the milk into a pitcher.

Melt the butter in a saucepan over a medium heat. Stir in the flour and cook, stirring, for 1 minute. Gradually add the milk, whisking constantly, then simmer over a low heat for 6–8 minutes, stirring occasionally until thickened. Stir in the lemon juice, mustard and chopped parsley and season the sauce well with salt and pepper.

Divide the fish pieces and raw shrimp between the pie dishes and spoon over the sauce to cover. Cover with plastic wrap and leave to cool.

Divide the pastry into 4 portions. Using one of the pie dishes as a guide, roll each piece out to a ¼-inch (3mm) thickness, about 1¼ inches (3cm) larger all round than the pie dishes. Cut a ¾-inch (2cm) wide strip from the outside of each rolled-out piece of pastry. Brush the rim of each pie dish with water and put the pastry strip on the rim, pressing it down and trimming the ends. Position the pastry lids to cover the pie filling and press the pastry edges together to seal.

Brush the pastry lids with the beaten egg to glaze and make a couple of slits in the center to let the steam escape. Bake for 30–35 minutes until the pastry is crisp and golden, and the filling is completely heated through.

Thai Chicken Pie

Serves 4–6

Thai food is one of my favorite cuisines and in this pie, creamy coconut and gently spiced chicken are topped with a lattice of shortcrust pastry – it's bound to be delicious! Serve me this with some fries and I'll be a happy man.

———

Shortcrust pastry

2 cups (250g) all-purpose flour, plus extra to dust

A pinch of fine salt

4 tbsp (60g) cold butter, diced

4 tbsp (60g) cold lard or vegetable shortening, diced

2–3 tbsp cold water

1 large egg, beaten, to glaze

Filling

2 skinless, boneless chicken thighs

2 skinless, boneless chicken breasts

2 tbsp coconut oil

2 shallots, finely chopped

2 garlic cloves, finely grated

1 red chile, seeded and finely chopped

1 tsp grated root ginger

2 tsp Thai green curry paste

Scant 1 cup (200g) unsweetened coconut cream

⅔ cup (150g) chicken broth

2 lime leaves

1 lemongrass stem, bruised

1 small sweet potato, about 6 oz (175g), peeled and cut into ½-inch (1cm) dice

1 tsp cornstarch, mixed with a splash of water

A splash of fish sauce

Start by making the filling. Cut all the chicken into 1-inch (1½cm) chunks and set aside. Heat the coconut oil in a sauté pan over a medium-low heat. Add the shallots, garlic, chile and ginger and fry until soft but not colored.

Stir in the curry paste and cook for a minute or two until the aroma is released. Add the chicken, increase the heat a little and cook, stirring, until it is sealed and no longer pink on the surface.

Add the coconut cream, chicken broth, lime leaves, lemongrass and sweet potato. Simmer for 12–15 minutes until the sweet potato is tender.

Stir in the cornstarch slurry and bring to a simmer, stirring constantly until the sauce begins to thicken. Remove from the heat and season with the fish sauce. Set aside to cool.

To make the shortcrust pastry, put the flour and salt into a large bowl. Add the diced butter and lard, or shortening, and rub in with your fingers until the mixture looks like fine breadcrumbs. Add just enough water to bring the dough together. Gently knead into a ball. Wrap in plastic wrap and chill for 30 minutes.

Heat your oven to 400°F. Remove and discard the lime leaves and lemongrass from the cooled pie filling. On a lightly floured surface, roll out two-thirds of the pastry and use to line an 8-inch (20cm) tart pan with removable base, 1¾ inches (4cm) deep. Roll out the remaining pastry to form a lid.

Spoon the cooled filling into the pie crust and brush the rim with beaten egg. Use a pastry lattice cutter to cut a pattern in the pastry lid. Gently pull the pastry to open up the lattice and position over the pie. Alternatively you could cut ½-inch (1cm) strips of pastry dough and arrange them in a lattice pattern on top of the pie. Press the edges down onto the rim of the pie dish to seal and trim away any excess pastry.

Brush the top of the pie with beaten egg and bake for 35–40 minutes until golden brown. Serve with stir-fried greens.

Steak and Mushroom Pot Pie

Serves 4–6

A true British classic, you can't mess with a traditional steak and mushroom pie. Packed with hearty flavors, generous chunks of meat and veggies, and a rich ale gravy, this is everything you could want in a pie. For best results, the ingredients for the puff pastry should be well chilled, so put the flours and water into the fridge with the butter an hour or so before you start.

———

Puff pastry

¾ cup plus 1 tbsp (100g) cold bread flour

1⅔ cups (200g) cold all-purpose flour, plus extra to dust

A pinch of fine salt

1 large egg, beaten

7 tbsp (100g) cold water

2 sticks plus 4 tbsp (300g) cold butter

To glaze

1 egg, beaten

Filling

1 tbsp sunflower oil

1¼ lb (500g) beef stew meat

1 onion, sliced

2 celery stalks, chopped

1 large carrot, chopped

2 tbsp all-purpose flour

2 sprigs of thyme

1 bay leaf

⅔ cup (150g) brown ale

2 cups (500g) beef broth

9 oz (250g) cremini mushrooms, halved

To make the puff pastry, combine the flours and salt in a large bowl. Add the beaten egg and two-thirds of the water and mix with a spoon for a minute. Add the remaining water and fold the sides of the dough into the middle, then turn the bowl 90° and repeat. Continue to fold the dough this way for 3 minutes until the water is fully incorporated and the dough is smooth.

Turn out onto a lightly floured surface and knead briefly. Form the dough into a rough rectangle, wrap in plastic wrap and put in the fridge to rest for an hour.

Using a rolling pin, bash the butter on a floured surface to flatten to a rectangle, 12 inches (30cm) long and just less then 8 inches (20cm) wide, about ½ inch (7mm) thick. Wrap in plastic wrap and chill in the fridge for 30 minutes.

Roll out the chilled dough to a rectangle, 18 x 8 inches (45 x 20cm). Lay the chilled butter on the dough so it covers the bottom two-thirds. Make sure it's positioned neatly and comes almost to the edges of the dough.

Lift the exposed dough at the top and fold down over half of the butter. Fold the butter-covered bottom half of the dough up over the top. You will now have a sandwich of two layers of butter and three of dough. Press or pinch the edges together to seal. Wrap in plastic wrap and chill in the fridge for an hour.

Remove the dough and turn it 90° so you have a short end towards you, then roll it into a rectangle, 18 x 8 inches (45 x 20cm). Fold one-third down, then fold the bottom third up over the top. Press or pinch the edges to seal.

Wrap the pastry in plastic wrap and chill for 1 hour. Repeat this stage of rolling, folding and chilling three more times.

Put the well-wrapped dough in the fridge to rest overnight (or for at least 6 hours) before using.

Continued overleaf

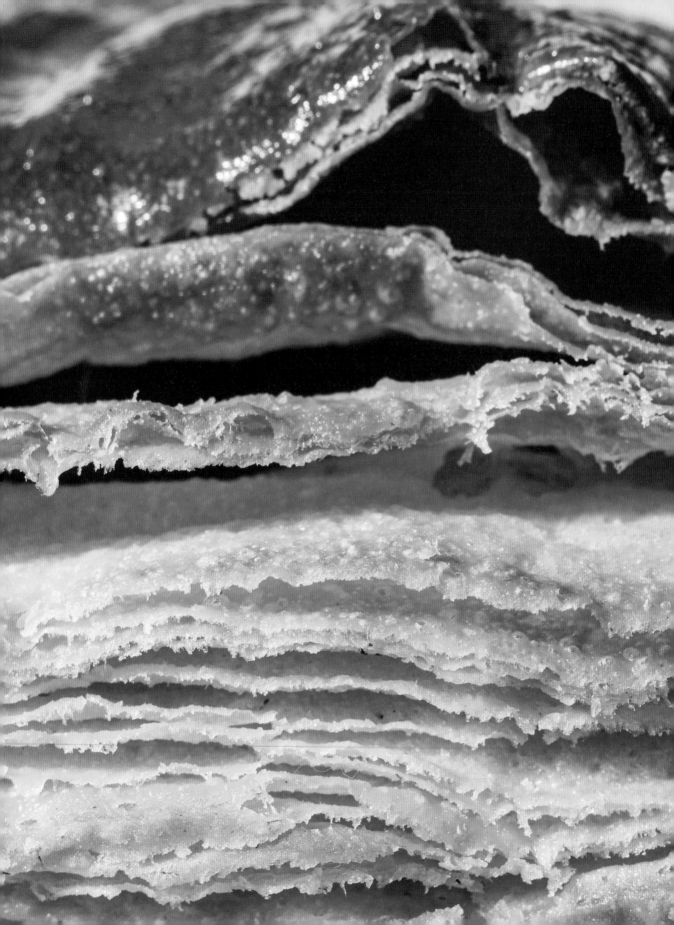

To prepare the filling, heat the oil in a large, wide sauté pan over a high heat. Brown the beef in two batches, turning to color evenly. Remove from the pan with a slotted spoon and set aside.

Add the onion, celery and carrot to the oil remaining in the pan and cook for a few minutes to soften, until starting to brown, then stir in the flour and cook, stirring, for a minute or two.

Return the meat and any resting juices to the pan. Add the thyme, bay leaf, ale and beef broth. Bring to a simmer, then lower the heat, put the lid on the pan and cook gently for 1½ hours until the meat is tender. Add the mushrooms and cook for a further 5 minutes.

Heat your oven to 400°F. Spoon the filling into a deep pie dish, roughly 9½ inches (24cm) in diameter, discarding the bay and thyme.

Roll out the pastry to a ¼-inch (5mm) thickness, about 1¼ inches (3cm) larger all round than the pie dish. Brush the rim of the dish with water then position the pastry lid over the filling. Trim away any overhanging pastry and press the edges down firmly onto the rim of the dish to seal.

Brush the pastry lid with beaten egg and make a couple of slits in the pie lid to let the steam escape. Bake the pie for 25–30 minutes until the pastry is risen and golden.

Meat and Potato Hand Pies

Makes 4

Sayers bakeries were all over the north-west of England when I was growing up in the seventies and individual beef and potato pies like these were one of their best-sellers. Meat and potato is a very traditional northern pairing and it always reminds me of going home.

———

Cheat's puff pastry

2⅓ cups plus 1 tbsp (300g)
all-purpose flour, plus
extra to dust

A pinch of fine salt

3 tbsp (50g) cold butter, diced

4–6 tbsp cold water

1 stick (120g) frozen butter

1 egg, beaten, to glaze

Filling

1 tbsp sunflower oil

9 oz (250g) ground beef

1 onion, finely diced

½ tbsp all-purpose flour

1 potato, peeled and diced

⅔ cup (150g) water

1 beef bouillon cube

A pinch of white pepper

To make the pastry, mix the flour and salt together in a bowl. Rub in the diced butter with your fingers until the mixture resembles breadcrumbs, then gradually incorporate enough water to form a dough.

On a lightly floured surface, roll out the dough to a rectangle, about 12 x 8 inches (30 x 20cm). Grate half the frozen butter over the bottom two-thirds of the dough. Fold down the top third then fold up the butter-topped bottom third of the dough, as if folding a letter.

Rotate the dough 90° and roll out to a rectangle, about 12 x 8 inches (30 x 20cm), again. Add the remaining frozen butter and fold, as before. Wrap in plastic wrap and put in the fridge for at least 30 minutes.

For the filling, heat the oil in a wide saucepan over a high heat. Add the ground beef and onion and cook until the meat begins to brown, stirring from time to time to break down any lumps of meat. Lower the heat, add the flour and cook, stirring, for 2–3 minutes.

Add the diced potato and water, then crumble in the bouillon cube and season with white pepper. Bring to a boil, then cover, lower the heat and simmer for 25 minutes, until the gravy thickens and the potato is tender. Taste and adjust the seasoning. Let cool then chill.

Heat your oven to 400°F and line a large baking sheet with parchment paper.

Divide the pastry into 8 equal pieces. On a lightly floured surface, roll into 5-inch (13cm) squares. Put 4 pastry squares on the prepared baking sheet and divide the cold filling between them, leaving a 1-inch (2½cm) border around the edge. Brush the pastry border with beaten egg then position the remaining pastry squares over the meat filling. Press the edges firmly to seal with a fork and trim to neaten.

Brush the pastry with beaten egg and bake for 25–30 minutes until the pastry is crisp and golden brown.

Pigs In Blankets

Makes 6

My first foray into baking was making pigs in blankets with my father in the bakery. Every morning we'd have a 'baker's breakfast': a soft floury roll with a pig in a blanket thrown in the middle. That was my breakfast for many years when I was learning the trade. These simple individual pigs in blankets, made with rough puff pastry and sausage meat, take me back to those days.

Rough puff pastry

1¾ cups plus 1 tbsp (225g) **all-purpose flour**, plus extra to dust

½ tsp **fine salt**

1 stick plus 5 tbsp (200g) cold **unsalted butter**, diced

Juice of ½ **lemon**

Up to scant 1 cup (180–200g) **cold water**

1 **egg**, beaten, to glaze

Filling

1 lb (450g) **sausage meat** (or your favorite sausages, skinned)

A pinch of **white pepper**

To make the pastry, put the flour, salt and butter into a bowl. Mix the lemon juice with the water and add three-quarters of the liquid to the bowl. Gently stir until the mixture comes together to form a lumpy dough, adding the remaining liquid if required (**1**). Don't knead or work too much – you want lumps of butter through the dough.

Tip the dough out onto a floured surface and flatten to a rectangle (**2**). Using a rolling pin, roll into a narrow rectangle around 1 inch (2½cm) thick. Fold one-third of the dough up on itself, then the opposite third down over that, as if folding a business letter (**3**). Wrap the pastry in plastic wrap and chill for at least 20 minutes.

Unwrap the pastry and repeat, turning the pastry 90° to the original folds (**4**) before you start rolling, to a rectangle 16 x 6 inches (40 x 15cm), then folding as before. Wrap and chill for 20 minutes. Repeat the process twice more, chilling the dough for at least 20 minutes between folds.

Heat your oven to 400°F and line a large baking sheet with parchment paper.

Roll out the pastry to a rectangle, 24 x 8 inches (60 x 20cm), and trim the edges to neaten. Cut into 6 even rectangles (**5**).

For the filling, mix the sausage meat with the white pepper. Divide the sausage meat into 6 equal portions. With lightly floured hands, roll each portion into a sausage shape, the width of the pastry rectangles. Lay a roll of sausage across each pastry rectangle, 2 inches (5cm) from one end. Brush the edges of the pastry with beaten egg and roll up to encase the sausage filling (**6**).

Put the pigs in blankets on the prepared baking sheets and brush with beaten egg. Bake for 30 minutes or until the pastry is golden and crisp and the sausage meat is cooked through. Leave to cool on a wire rack for 5 minutes before serving.

Steps illustrated overleaf

5

6

The Ultimate Sausage Roll

Serves 6

Sausage roll is the British name for pigs in blankets and this is my ultimate jumbo-sized version. The addition of Stilton gives it a bit of a kick, but if you prefer you could use less Stilton and cook another onion instead – sprinkle the extra caramelized onion directly on the pastry for extra sweetness before you roll it up.

———

Rough puff pastry

1¾ cups plus 1 tbsp (225g) **all-purpose flour**, plus extra to dust

½ tsp **fine salt**

1 stick plus 5 tbsp (200g) **cold unsalted butter**, diced

Juice of ½ **lemon**

Up to scant 1 cup (180–200g) **cold water**

Filling

1 tbsp **oil**

1 small **onion**, finely diced

14 oz (400g) **sausage meat** (or your favorite sausages, skinned)

1¼ cups (125g) **crumbled Stilton**, or similar blue cheese

1 tbsp **thyme leaves**

A pinch of **white pepper**

To finish

2 **egg yolks**, beaten, to glaze

2 tsp **nigella seeds**

2 tsp **sesame seeds**

To make the pastry, put the flour, salt and butter into a bowl. Mix the lemon juice with the water and add three-quarters of the liquid to the bowl. Gently stir until the mixture comes together to form a lumpy dough, adding the remaining liquid if required. Don't knead or work too much – you want lumps of butter through the dough.

Tip the dough onto a floured surface and flatten to a rectangle. Using a rolling pin, roll into a narrow rectangle around 1 inch (2½cm) thick. Fold one-third of the dough up on itself, then the opposite third down over that, as if folding a business letter. Wrap the pastry in plastic wrap and chill for at least 20 minutes.

Unwrap the pastry and repeat, rolling the pastry at 90° to the original roll, to a rectangle 16 x 6 inches (40 x 15cm), then folding as before. Wrap and chill for 20 minutes. Repeat the process twice more, chilling the dough for at least 20 minutes between folds.

Heat your oven to 400°F and line a large baking sheet with parchment paper.

For the filling, heat the oil in a small frying pan over a medium heat, add the onion and cook for 7–10 minutes until softened and just turning golden brown. Leave to cool. In a bowl, mix the sausage meat with the cooled onion, crumbled Stilton, thyme and white pepper.

With floured hands, roll the filling into an 8-inch (20cm) long sausage and wrap tightly in plastic wrap. Chill for 30 minutes.

Roll out the pastry to a rectangle, 12 x 8 inches (30 x 20cm), and trim the edges to neaten. Put on the baking sheet and chill for 20 minutes.

Continued overleaf

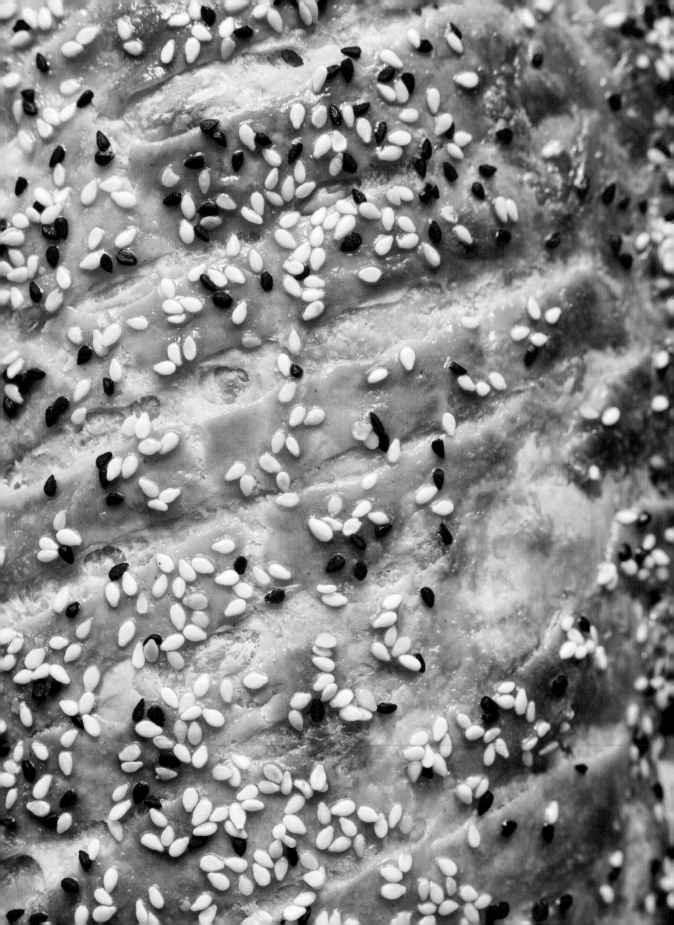

Unwrap the sausage and lay it along the pastry rectangle, 2½ inches (6cm) from one edge. Brush the exposed pastry with beaten egg yolk, leaving the 2½-inch (6cm) border clear. Fold the egg-washed pastry over the sausage filling to meet the border and encase the sausage filling. Press the edges firmly together. Press a floured fork firmly along the length of the sealed edge. (You may need to keep dipping the fork in flour to stop it sticking.)

Brush the sausage roll all over with more egg and score the pastry on the diagonal. Chill for 15 minutes. Heat your oven to 415°F.

Brush the pastry again with egg, all over, then sprinkle with the nigella and sesame seeds. Bake for 30 minutes or until the pastry is golden and crisp and the sausage meat is cooked through.

Leave to cool on a wire rack for 10 minutes before slicing. Serve with your favorite relishes and chutneys.

Cheese and Onion Pasties

Makes 4

It's all about strong flavors and contrasting textures in this classic British savory hand pie. As a kid, a cheese and onion pasty was a close second to pigs in blankets for me. In this version, the tang from the onion and chives, and the richness from the Cheddar and cream cheese filling – all contrasting with the buttery flaky pastry – is unbelievably delicious. These pasties are also very simple to make.

———

Shortcrust pastry

3⅔ cups (450g) all-purpose flour, plus extra to dust

½ tsp fine salt

7 tbsp (100g) cold unsalted butter, diced

7 tbsp (100g) cold lard or vegetable shortening, diced

About ⅓ cup (90g) cold water

1 egg, beaten, to glaze

Filling

1 tbsp vegetable oil

2 tbsp (25g) unsalted butter

1 large onion, finely diced

1 waxy potato, about 11 oz (300g), peeled and cut into ½-inch (1cm) dice

2 cups (200g) grated sharp Cheddar

5 tbsp (75g) cream cheese

2 tbsp chopped chives

Sea salt and white pepper

To make the pastry, mix the flour and salt together in a large bowl. Add the diced butter and lard, or shortening, and rub in with your fingers until the mixture resembles breadcrumbs. Add just enough water to bring the mixture together and form a firm dough. Knead briefly until smooth. Wrap in plastic wrap and chill for 30 minutes.

For the filling, heat the oil and butter together in a frying pan. Add the onion and cook over a medium-low heat for about 10 minutes until soft but not colored, stirring from time to time. Add the diced potato, with a splash of water, and cook for 5–10 minutes. Take off the heat and set aside to cool.

Heat your oven to 400°F and line two baking sheets with parchment paper.

Divide the pastry into 4 equal pieces. On a lightly floured surface, roll out each piece to a large round, ⅛ inch (3mm) thick. Using a plate as a guide, trim each to a neat circle, 10 inches (24cm) in diameter.

Add the grated Cheddar, cream cheese and chopped chives to the onion and potato and stir to combine. Season well with salt and white pepper.

Pile a quarter of the filling onto one half of each pastry circle, leaving a 1¼-inch (3cm) border around the edge. Brush the border with a little beaten egg, then fold the other half of the pastry over to enclose the filling, making sure the edges meet. Press the edges firmly together and crimp them or press with a floured fork.

Put the pasties on the prepared baking sheets. Cut a couple of small slits in the middle of each one and brush with beaten egg. Bake for 20 minutes, then lower the oven setting to 325°F and bake for a further 25 minutes.

Eat hot from the oven, with your favorite relish or baked beans.

Hand-raised
Sunday Lunch Pie

Serves 8

Hand-raised pies were very popular in Tudor England and this one – layered with chicken, sausage meat and dried apricots – reflects the flavors of a traditional British Sunday roast lunch. The hot water crust pastry is robust and waterproof, sealing in the filling. You need to work quite quickly with the hot pastry so it doesn't chill and set before you've lined the pan.

———

Hot water crust pastry

3⅔ cups (450g) all-purpose flour

¾ cup (100g) bread flour

1 tsp fine salt

5 tbsp (75g) cold butter, diced

¾ cup plus 1 tbsp (200g) water

7 tbsp (100g) lard or vegetable shortening, plus extra to grease the pan

1 egg, beaten, to glaze

Filling

2 cups (500g) of your favorite stuffing or dressing (not too moist)

1 lb (450g) sausage meat

3½ cups (250g) shredded cooked chicken (white and dark meat)

⅓ cup (50g) dried apricots, chopped

Heat your oven to 400°F. Grease a deep 8-inch (20cm) springform pan with lard or vegetable shortening.

To make the pastry, mix the flours and salt together in a large bowl, then add the butter and rub in with your fingers. In a saucepan, heat the water with the lard, or shortening, until it just boils. Immediately pour the hot liquid onto the flour and mix together vigorously with a wooden spoon. Tip onto a lightly floured surface and knead until smooth.

Working quickly, divide the pastry into two-thirds and one-third. Roll out the larger piece of dough and use to line the prepared pan, leaving the excess pastry hanging over the sides. Roll out the remaining pastry to form a lid.

Spoon half of the stuffing into the pie crust, pressing it down evenly with the back of a spoon. Add half of the sausage meat and press down to form an even layer. Arrange the chicken over the sausage meat and scatter over the apricots. Top with another layer of sausage meat and then a final layer of stuffing.

Brush the overhanging pastry edges with water. Position the lid over the top of the filling and squeeze the pastry edges together to seal. Trim off any excess pastry and crimp the edges, by pressing the pastry outwards with one finger between the thumb and forefinger of your other hand all round to create a fluted edge.

Decorate the top with leaves or other shapes cut from the pastry trimmings. Brush the top of the pie with beaten egg and make a few slits in the center.

Stand the pan on a baking sheet and bake for 30 minutes, then lower the oven setting to 325°F and bake for 45 minutes. Leave the pie to cool in the pan for 30 minutes before carefully unmolding. Serve hot with vegetables of your choice, or cold with chutney or relishes.

Beef Empanadas

Makes 9

I made these sweet and warmly spiced beef empanadas while filming in Madrid. We visited a food market in the city center and tasted so many amazing little pastries. Making and eating these always reminds me of that fascinating trip.

————

Pastry

2¼ cups plus 1 tbsp (300g) all-purpose flour

A pinch of fine salt

1 stick plus 2 tbsp (150g) butter, melted

1 large egg, beaten

2–3 tbsp warm water

1 egg yolk, beaten, to glaze

Filling

1 tbsp vegetable oil

10 oz (300g) ground beef

1 small onion, finely chopped

1 red bell pepper, cored, seeded and finely chopped

1 garlic clove, finely chopped

½ tsp cumin seeds

A pinch of crushed red pepper flakes

1 tbsp tomato paste

1 beef bouillon cube

7 tbsp (100g) water

1 tbsp raisins

Sea salt and black pepper

To make the pastry, mix the flour and salt together in a bowl. Add the melted butter and beaten egg and stir to mix, then add just enough warm water to bring the mixture together and form a firm dough. Turn out onto a clean surface and knead for 5 minutes until smooth. Wrap in plastic wrap and set aside at room temperature while you make the filling.

Heat most of the oil in a large wide-based saucepan. Add the ground beef and cook, stirring to break up any lumps, until browned; remove with a slotted spoon to a plate and put to one side.

Add a little more oil to the pan and cook the onion for a few minutes until it begins to soften. Add the red bell pepper, garlic, cumin seeds and red pepper flakes and cook gently for 10 minutes.

Return the beef to the pan and stir in the tomato paste. Crumble in the bouillon cube, pour in the water and add the raisins. Simmer for 5 minutes then remove from the heat. Taste the filling and adjust the seasoning with salt and pepper. Leave to cool.

Heat your oven to 400°F and line a large baking sheet with parchment paper.

Roll out the pastry on a lightly floured surface to a ⅛-inch (3mm) thickness. Using an inverted small bowl, measuring about 6 inches (15cm) in diameter across the top, as a guide, cut out 9 circles.

Divide the filling between the pastry discs, leaving a 1-inch (2–3cm) clear border around the edge. Dampen the pastry border with water and fold over one half to make a semi-circular parcel. Press the edges together firmly and crimp or press the edges with a floured fork.

Put the empanadas on the prepared baking sheet and brush with beaten egg. Bake for 20–25 minutes or until golden brown. Best eaten warm from the oven.

Apple Pie

Depending on where you are in the world, the apple pie you are familiar with will look different, ranging from a deep-dish pie to something more like a French apple tart. I grew up with double-crust apple pies made in a pie plate, like this one. My mother used to make this pie using sharp apples from her tree in the garden, with plenty of sugar to sweeten them. I like to use a mixture of apples in my pie filling, both sweet and sharp, with some providing a fluffy texture as they cook and others giving crunch. Cornstarch dusted on the base of the pie crust is a good trick to help prevent a soggy bottom.

———

Pastry
2¼ cups (275g) all-purpose flour

2 tbsp confectioners' sugar

1 stick plus 2 tbsp (140g) cold butter, diced

3–4 tbsp cold water

Filling
3 large Granny Smith apples

2 McIntosh or Pink Lady apples

Juice of 1 lemon

2 tbsp (25g) unsalted butter

4 tbsp superfine sugar

1 cinnamon stick

2 tbsp cornstarch

Glaze
1 large egg, beaten

2 tsp superfine sugar

To make the pastry, mix the flour and confectioners' sugar together in a bowl. Add the diced butter and rub in with your fingers until the mixture resembles fine breadcrumbs. Using a dinner knife, work in just enough water to bring the dough together. Gently knead into a ball, wrap in plastic wrap and put in the fridge to rest while you make the filling.

Peel and core the apples, reserving the peel and cores. Cut all the apples into slices, about ¼ inch (5mm) thick. Sprinkle lemon juice over the prepared apples to prevent browning.

Put the apple peel and cores into a saucepan and pour on cold water to cover. Bring to a boil, lower the heat and simmer for 15 minutes. Take off the heat and leave to cool. Strain the cooled apple liquid to remove the peel and cores.

Put the McIntosh apples in a saucepan with the butter, sugar, cinnamon stick and 3 tablespoons of the apple liquid. Cook gently over a low heat, stirring occasionally, until the apples soften but still hold their shape. Leave to cool. Remove and discard the cinnamon stick.

Fold the sliced Granny Smith apples through the cooked apple, along with another 3 tablespoons of the apple liquid.

Heat your oven to 400°F and have a 9-inch (24cm) pie plate ready.

Divide the pastry into two pieces: roughly two-thirds and one-third. On a floured surface, roll out the larger piece to a ⅛ inch (2–3mm) thickness. Use this to line the base of the pie plate. Roll out the remaining pastry to form the lid of the pie.

Continued overleaf

Sprinkle the cornstarch over the pie crust base then spoon the cooled apple filling evenly over the top.

Brush the pastry edges with some of the beaten egg (you'll use the rest for the glaze), then position the pastry lid over the filling. Crimp the edges by pressing the pastry outwards with one finger between the thumb and forefinger of your other hand all round to create a fluted edge, or simply press with a floured fork. Trim away any excess pastry.

Use the pastry trimmings to make leaves or other decorations, sticking them on top of the pie with a little of the egg glaze.

Brush the pastry lid with beaten egg and then sprinkle with the superfine sugar to glaze. Make three small slits in the top to let the steam out. Bake the pie for 30–35 minutes until the pastry is golden brown.

Leave the pie to rest for 15 minutes before serving. Enjoy it warm with ice cream, cream or crème anglaise.

Pear and Almond Slices

In this recipe, a sweetened pie crust is filled with a creamy almond frangipane and topped with sliced fresh pear. A hidden layer of ginger preserves on the base provides extra depth and subtle heat.

Makes 8–10

Pastry

1⅔ cups (200g) all-purpose flour

2 tbsp confectioners' sugar

7 tbsp (100g) cold butter, diced

1 large egg, beaten

1 tsp lemon juice

2–3 tsp cold water

Filling

7 tbsp (100g) unsalted butter

½ cup (100g) superfine sugar

2 large eggs

⅓ cup plus 1 tbsp (50g) all-purpose flour

¾ cup (75g) almond flour

A dash of almond extract

½ cup (125g) ginger preserves

2 ripe, firm dessert pears

To finish

3 tbsp (20g) sliced almonds

Confectioners' sugar, to dust

To make the pastry, mix the flour and confectioners' sugar together in a large bowl and add the butter. Using your fingers, rub the butter into the flour mix until the mixture resembles fine breadcrumbs. Add the egg and lemon juice and mix in, using a dinner knife. Now mix in the water, 1 tsp at a time, until the pastry comes together, adding just as much as you need to form a dough.

Knead the pastry gently to form a smooth ball then wrap in parchment paper or plastic wrap and chill for 20 minutes.

Heat your oven to 400°F. On a lightly floured surface, roll out the pastry to a ⅛-inch (3mm) thickness and use to line a 13 x 4-inch (32 x 10cm) rectangular tart pan with a removable base (**1**). Leave the excess pastry overhanging the edges of the pan. Stand the pan on a baking sheet.

Line the pie crust with parchment paper, add a layer of baking beans and bake 'blind' for 12–15 minutes. Remove the paper and beans (**2**) and return to the oven for 5 minutes until the pastry base is very lightly colored. Remove from the oven and lower the oven temperature to 350°F. Use a small, sharp knife to trim away the excess pastry from the edge of the pan.

For the filling, to make the frangipane, beat the butter and sugar together in a large bowl until light and fluffy, then beat in the eggs, one at a time. Stir in the all-purpose flour, almond flour and almond extract.

Spread the ginger preserves over the base of the pie crust. Top with the frangipane and spread evenly (**3**). Halve, core and thinly slice the pears then arrange overlapping on the frangipane, gently pushing them in (**4**).

Bake for 10 minutes, then scatter the sliced almonds over the surface and bake for another 15 minutes until golden. Leave to cool completely in the pan.

Cut the tart into slices and carefully remove from the pan. Dust with confectioners' sugar before serving.

Steps illustrated overleaf

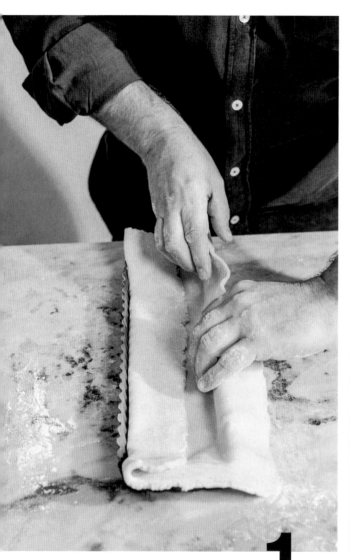

3

4

Key Lime Pie

Serves 6

When I was in Miami a few years ago, I made this pie using local key limes. I was petrified of it not working out, but thankfully the hotel chef came over and gave me the thumbs up! Here I have adapted the recipe for regular limes, but if you can get key limes then use ⅓ cup (90g) freshly squeezed juice and 2 tablespoons of finely grated zest in the filling, and the finely grated zest of one key lime to finish.

———

Base
8 oz (about 14 sheets/225g) graham crackers
1 stick (125g) butter, melted

Put the graham crackers in a food processor and pulse to a crumb-like texture (not too fine). Tip into a bowl, add the melted butter and stir to combine.

Spoon the crumb mix into an 8-inch (20cm) tart pan with removable base, 1¼ inches (3cm) deep. Press it evenly onto the base and push the mixture up the sides of the pan to create a crust. Put in the fridge for 30 minutes or so to set.

Filling
4 large egg yolks
1 x 14-oz (397g) can sweetened condensed milk
Finely grated zest and juice of 4 limes

Heat your oven to 350°F.

To make the filling, whisk the egg yolks with the sweetened condensed milk. Add the lime zest and juice and whisk again to combine.

Pour the filling into the prepared crust and bake for 25–30 minutes or until risen and just set. The filling may have started to color around the edges.

Leave the pie to cool in the pan then chill for at least 2 hours before serving.

To finish
200g heavy cream
Finely grated zest of 1 lime

When you're ready to serve, whip the heavy cream until holding (not quite stiff) peaks and put in a pastry bag fitted with a ½-inch (1cm) fluted tip. Pipe the cream around the edge of the pie filling and finish with a scattering of lime zest.

Pecan Pie

Crossing America on a motorbike from New York to LA, we made a stop down south in Georgia where I tried an amazing pecan pie in a bakery. It's such an American classic. Laden with dark brown sugar, golden syrup and molasses, it is quite sweet, with a buttery richness, and has lots of texture from the pecans. I like to serve it with a scoop of vanilla ice cream or a pitcher of pouring cream. The little bit of cream cheese in the pie crust adds a subtle acidity and color.

———

Pastry

1⅔ cups (200g) all-purpose flour, plus extra to dust

A pinch of fine salt

5 tbsp (75g) cold butter, diced

1 large egg yolk

3 tbsp (50g) cream cheese

2–3 tbsp cold water

Filling

1½ cups (150g) pecan nuts

5 tbsp (80g) butter

⅔ cup (120g) dark brown sugar

½ cup (150g) Lyle's golden syrup

3 tbsp (60g) molasses

1½ tbsp cornstarch

1 large egg, beaten

1 extra egg yolk

¾ cup (175g) heavy cream

To make the pastry, mix the flour and salt together in a bowl. Add the butter and rub in lightly with your fingers until the mixture resembles fine breadcrumbs. Add the egg yolk and cream cheese. Stir into the mixture with a dinner knife, then add the water, 1 tablespoon at a time. Only add enough to bring the pastry together; you may not need all of it.

When the dough begins to hold together, gently knead it into a smooth ball. Wrap in plastic wrap and chill for at least 30 minutes.

Heat your oven to 400°F. On a lightly floured surface, roll out the pastry to a ⅛-inch (3mm) thickness and use to line a 9-inch (23cm) loose-bottomed tart pan, leaving a little excess hanging over the edge of the pan.

Line the pie crust with parchment paper and fill with a layer of baking beans. Bake 'blind' for 12–15 minutes, until the pastry is dry to the touch. Remove the paper and beans and return the pie crust to the oven for about 5 minutes until it is very lightly colored. Use a small, sharp knife to trim away the excess pastry from the edge.

Lower the oven temperature to 325°F. Scatter the pecan nuts on a baking sheet and toast in the oven for 8–10 minutes, keeping a close eye to make sure they don't burn. Tip onto a plate and leave to cool. Finely chop half of the pecans. Increase the oven temperature to 350°F.

To make the filling, melt the butter, sugar, syrup and molasses together in a saucepan over a medium-low heat. Whisk in the cornstarch and stir over the heat until smooth and thickened. Take off the heat and add the beaten egg, extra egg yolk and cream. Mix well then stir in the chopped pecans.

Pour the filling into the cooked pie crust and arrange the remaining pecans on top. Bake for 30–35 minutes until the filling is risen and just set. Leave to cool completely in the pan, then remove and serve with ice cream or cream.

Croissants

Makes 20

One of the first things I learned to make when working in hotels was a good croissant and it has always stuck with me. There are quite a few stages to the process, but I really think it's worth the effort, plus you can control what goes into them and the kind of butter you use. Choose one with a full flavor. I love making croissants and usually have some dough in the freezer ready to go.

Dough

4 cups (500g) bread flour, plus extra to dust

1¼ tsp (10g) fine salt

¼ cup (50g) superfine sugar

3¾ tsp (10g) instant dried yeast

1 cup plus 2 tbsp (280g) cold water

2 sticks plus 4 tbsp (300g) cold unsalted butter (good-quality)

1 egg, beaten, to glaze

———

To prepare the dough, in a large bowl, mix the flour, salt, sugar and yeast together. Add three-quarters of the water and stir together to combine, then start folding the sides of the dough into the middle for 1 minute, turning the bowl as you do so. Add the remaining water and continue to fold in the sides of the dough for 3 minutes, turning the bowl 90° each time.

Tip the dough onto a lightly floured surface and knead well for 10 minutes. Put the dough back in the bowl, cover with plastic wrap and leave to rise at room temperature for 1 hour.

Tip the dough out, knead to knock the air out and shape into a ball. Put back in the bowl, cover the bowl with plastic wrap and put in the fridge for 2 hours.

Tip the dough out and roll into a rectangle, about 20 x 8 inches (50 x 20cm), with a short side facing you (**1**). Take your butter from the fridge and coat in a little flour then, using a rolling pin, flatten to a rectangle 13 x 8 inches (33 x 20cm). Put the butter on the dough to cover the two-thirds closest to you (**2**). Make sure it fits to the edges of the dough all the way up, leaving the top one-third of the dough exposed. Fold this top third down over the butter, then fold the bottom (butter-topped) third on top. You should now have two layers of butter and three layers of dough. Wrap in plastic wrap and chill for 2 hours.

Unwrap your dough, turn it 90° (so the exposed butter edge is towards you) (**3**) and roll out on a lightly floured surface to a 20 x 8-inch (50 x 20cm) rectangle again. Fold up the bottom third of the dough, then fold the top third down over the top. Wrap again and chill for 1 hour. Repeat this process three more times, chilling for an hour in between each sequence.

Finally, wrap the croissant dough well and put in the fridge to rest overnight (or for 6–7 hours); or freeze for future use.

Continued overleaf

When you are ready to shape the croissants, line two large baking sheets with parchment paper. Roll out your dough to a 24 x 12-inch (60 x 30cm) rectangle, about ¼ inch (6mm) thick. Using a pizza cutter, cut the rectangle in half lengthwise (**4**).

Lay the pastry strips lengthwise in front of you. Cut a triangle from one of the pastry edges, 4–4½ inches (10–11cm) across the base and tapering down to a point. Use this first triangle as a size guide to cutting the rest. You should get 10 triangles out of each strip.

Put each pastry triangle with the point towards you and hold it firmly with one hand (**5**). Starting at the thick end, roll each one up to resemble a croissant (**6**). You can also freeze the croissant at this stage for future use.

Put the croissants on the prepared baking sheets, leaving space in between for them to rise. Put each baking sheet in a roomy freezer bag and leave to proof for 2 hours.

Heat your oven to 415°F. Brush the croissants with beaten egg and bake for 15–20 minutes, until golden brown. Transfer to a wire rack to cool slightly. Best eaten while still warm.

Steps continued overleaf

1

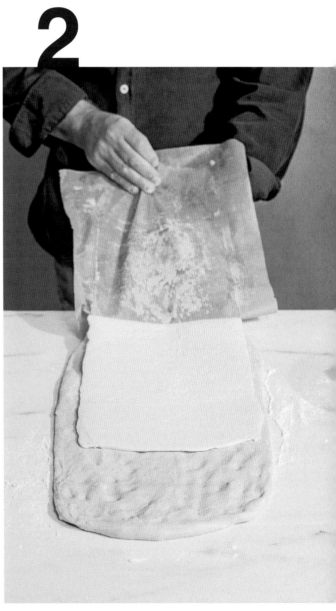

2

3

4

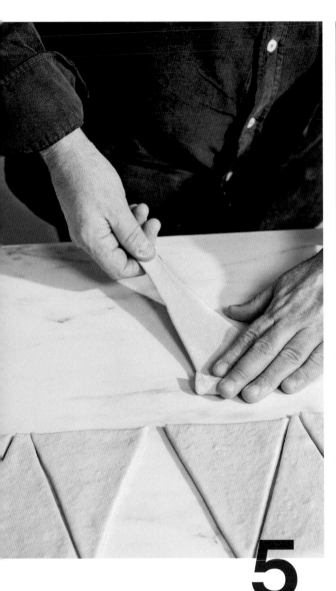

5

6

Pain au Chocolat

Fresh-from-the-oven pain au chocolat is an experience everyone should try. Since you're taking the time to make these from scratch, think carefully about the chocolate you use. And use good-quality butter. Having said that, feel free to use white, bittersweet or milk chocolate, or even stick some of your favorite chocolate bar in there if you fancy that in the morning!

1 quantity croissant dough (see page 234), rested overnight in the fridge

32 chocolate batons, 3–3½ inches (7–9cm) long (good-quality)

1 egg, beaten, to glaze

When you are ready to shape the pain au chocolat, line two large baking sheets with parchment paper. Unwrap your croissant dough and roll out on a lightly floured surface to a rectangle, about ¼ inch (5mm) thick.

Cut into smaller rectangles, about 3 x 4 inches (7 x 10cm). Put a chocolate baton across the shorter side of each rectangle, about 1¼ inches (3cm) from the edge and fold the pastry edge over to cover it, then put the second baton on the pastry and fold over again to make a parcel.

Put the pastries, seam side down, on the prepared baking sheets. Put each baking sheet in a freezer bag and leave to proof for 2 hours.

Heat your oven to 400°F. Brush the pain au chocolat with the beaten egg and bake for 20 minutes, or until golden brown. Transfer to a wire rack to cool slightly. Best eaten while still warm.

Apricot Danish Pastries

Makes 15

I love crème anglaise and would happily eat it with almost any pastry or dessert. Combining a vanilla crème pât with flaky pastry and sweet apricots makes this my number one choice for a mid-morning treat. Yes, the pastries take a bit of preparation, but they are totally worth the effort – trust me, they're so much better than any you can buy. You can also freeze the dough; simply thaw it in the fridge overnight whenever you want to bake a batch of these.

———

Danish pastry

4 cups (500g) bread flour

1 tsp (8g) fine salt

¼ cup (50g) superfine sugar

2 large eggs

3¾ tsp (10g) instant dried yeast

5 tbsp (80g) cold water

⅓ cup (90g) tepid whole milk

2 sticks plus 3 tbsp (280g) cold unsalted butter (good-quality)

1 egg, beaten, to glaze

Crème pâtissière

¾ cup (180g) whole milk

3 tbsp (50g) heavy cream

2 tsp vanilla bean paste

4 large egg yolks

⅓ cup (70g) superfine sugar

2½ tbsp (25g) cornstarch

3 tbsp (40g) unsalted butter, in pieces

Apricot topping and glaze

⅔ cup (150g) apricot preserves

1 x 15-oz (400g) can apricot halves, drained

Glacé icing

1 cup (100g) confectioners' sugar, sifted

Finely grated zest of 1 lemon

2 tbsp (30g) water

To make the pastry, in a large bowl, mix the flour, salt, sugar, eggs and yeast together. Add the water and milk and stir together to combine, then start folding the sides of the dough into the middle for 1 minute, turning the bowl as you do so. Continue to fold in the sides of the dough for a further 3 minutes.

Transfer the dough to a lightly floured surface and knead well for 10 minutes. Put the dough back in the bowl, cover with plastic wrap and leave to rise at room temperature for 1 hour.

Tip the dough out, knead to knock the air out and shape into a ball. Put back in the bowl, cover the bowl with plastic wrap and put in the fridge for 2 hours.

Tip the dough out and roll into a rectangle, about 20 x 8 inches (50 x 20cm), with a short side facing you. Coat the butter in a little flour then, using a rolling pin, flatten to a rectangle 13 x 8 inches (33 x 20cm). Put the butter on the dough to cover the two-thirds closest to you. Make sure it fits to the edges of the dough all the way up, leaving the top one-third exposed. Fold this top third down over the butter, then fold the bottom (butter-topped) third on top. You should now have two layers of butter and three layers of dough. Wrap in plastic wrap and chill for 2 hours.

Unwrap your dough, turn it so the exposed butter edge is towards you and roll out on a lightly floured surface to a 20 x 8 inches (50 x 20cm) rectangle again. Fold up the bottom third of the dough, then fold the top third down over the top. Wrap again and chill for 1 hour. Repeat this turning, rolling, folding and chilling sequence three more times.

Finally, wrap the pastry dough well and put in the fridge to rest overnight (or for 6–7 hours); or freeze for future use.

Continued overleaf

Line two large baking sheets with parchment paper. Unwrap your Danish pastry dough and roll out on a lightly floured surface to a rectangle, about 20 x 12 inches (50 x 30cm) and ¼ inch (7mm) thick. Cut the dough into 4-inch (10cm) squares (you should have 15). Fold the opposite corners of each square into the middle to form a smaller square.

Lay the pastry squares on the lined baking sheets, leaving space in between for them to expand and put each baking sheet in a large, roomy freezer bag. Leave to rise at room temperature for 2–3 hours, or overnight in the fridge.

While the dough is rising, make your crème pâtissière. In a saucepan over a low heat, warm the milk, cream and vanilla bean paste together and slowly bring to a boil. Meanwhile, in a bowl, whisk the egg yolks with the sugar and cornstarch until smoothly combined. As the milk mixture starts to come to a boil, pour a little onto the whisked mixture, stirring well. Pour on the rest of the milk mix, whisking as you do so.

Pour the mixture back into the saucepan and bring to a simmer over a medium-low heat. Cook, stirring continuously, until the crème pâtissière is thickened. Pass through a strainer into a bowl, add the butter and stir until melted. Cover the surface with plastic wrap to prevent a skin forming and leave to cool.

Once the pastry squares are risen, heat your oven to 415°F. Put your crème pâtissière into a pastry bag fitted with a ½-inch (1cm) tip and pipe a good spoonful into the middle of each pastry square. Brush the pastry around the filling with beaten egg and bake for 20 minutes until risen and golden brown.

Meanwhile, for the glaze, in a small pan heat the apricot preserves with a good splash of water until simmering.

When you take the pastries from the oven, put an apricot half on the crème pâtissière in the center of each pastry and generously brush the pastries with the warm apricot preserves to glaze. Transfer to a wire rack to cool.

To finish, mix the confectioners' sugar with the lemon zest and water to make a thin, glossy icing. Brush over the sides of the pastries, leave to set and then devour!

Pains aux Raisins

Makes 15

It's the glacé icing, flavored with mandarin or clementine, brushed over these pains aux raisins that really sets them apart – that and the perfect ratio of crème pâtissière to buttery pastry. Get them ready to bake the day before and put them in the oven in the morning. Your guests will be blown away.

———

1 quantity Danish pastry dough (see page 242), rested overnight in the fridge

1 quantity crème pâtissière (see page 242), cooled

1½ cups (230g) raisins

2 tsp ground cinnamon

1 egg, beaten, to glaze

⅔ cup (200g) apricot preserves, to glaze

Icing

1 cup (100g) confectioners' sugar, sifted

Finely grated zest of 2 mandarins or satsumas

2 tbsp (30g) water

When you are ready to shape the pains aux raisins, line two large baking sheets with parchment paper.

Roll out your Danish pastry dough on a lightly floured surface to a rectangle, about 24 x 12 inches (60 x 30cm). Have a long side closest to you and tack this to the table, by pressing it down lightly, to hold it in place.

Spread the crème pâtissière evenly on top of the pastry rectangle, leaving a ½-inch (1cm) clear border along the edges. Scatter the raisins over the surface and sprinkle evenly with the ground cinnamon.

Starting from the long edge furthest from you, start to roll up the dough, like a jelly roll, tugging it gently as you do so to create some tension. Once the roll is complete, roll it back and forth on the table to seal the join.

Now cut the pastry roll into 1½-inch (4cm) thick slices. Lay these, cut side up, on the prepared baking sheets, leaving space in between for them to expand. Put each baking sheet in a large, roomy freezer bag. Leave to rise at room temperature for 2–3 hours, or overnight in the fridge.

Once the pastry spirals are risen, heat your oven to 415°F. Brush the pastries with beaten egg and bake for 20–25 minutes until they are risen and golden brown.

Heat the apricot preserves with a good splash of water in a pan until simmering. When you take the pastries from the oven, generously brush the top of each with the warm apricot preserves to glaze. Transfer the pastries to a wire rack to cool.

Mix the confectioners' sugar with the clementine zest and water to make a thin, glossy icing. Brush this over the pastries and leave to set before serving.

5

6

7

Desserts

It's no secret that I have a bit of a sweet tooth, so choosing the short-list for this chapter was a bit of a challenge. Probably more so than any other category of baking, desserts cover a huge range of styles and techniques, from the very simple to the over-the-top elaborate. But what they all have in common is that they're about pure enjoyment. A dessert is always a welcome extra at the end of a meal, and so if you've decided you are going to have one, don't be apologetic about it. This is not a time to be thinking of healthy alternatives.

We've been enjoying sweet treats for centuries and I've included some really old-fashioned British classic recipes, like bread pudding and steamed lemon sponges (pages 269 and 256). I've also shared what will be the best sticky toffee pudding you've ever tasted on page 254. That's what desserts are to me – mostly wintry, warming, filling and on just the right side of stodgy.

That doesn't mean you can't enjoy a dessert during the summer though, and meringues make the perfect hot-weather option. You can keep things really simple and serve them with just whipped cream, which is how my grandmother used to serve her meringues and is how I have on page 288. Or you can turn them into a fruit pavlova or mango roulade (pages 276 and 278) for something a bit fresher. Crisp on the outside and with that chewy mallow middle, a well-made meringue is a thing of perfection.

Making a dessert can be a great opportunity to show off, too. Combining different skills and elements can produce works of art. If you're up for testing your abilities, the chocolate and raspberry entremets on page 290 takes desserts up a level. It can be a bit stagey to prepare these kinds of bakes, but each individual step is usually straightforward; it's just about timing and patience. Take your time and stick with it for a true showstopper of a dessert.

Desserts should be an all-round treat, so take as much pleasure in making them as you do in eating them.

Sticky Toffee Pudding

Serves 9

A real crowd-pleaser of a dessert, sticky toffee pudding is surprisingly easy to make. It's essentially a date sponge covered in a rich toffee sauce then warmed under the broiler. Serve it with pouring cream or ice cream for that irresistible hot-cold contrast.

————

1 cup (175g) chopped pitted dates

¾ cup plus 1 tbsp (200g) boiling water

1 tsp baking soda

5 tbsp (75g) unsalted butter, plus extra to grease the pan

¾ cup (150g) dark brown sugar

2 large eggs, beaten

1⅓ cups plus 1 tbsp (175g) all-purpose flour

2¾ tsp baking powder

Sticky toffee sauce

7 tbsp (100g) unsalted butter, diced

¾ cup (150g) dark brown sugar

⅔ cup (150g) heavy cream

Heat your oven to 350°F and butter a 9 x 11-inch (23 x 28cm) baking pan, 1½ inches (4cm) deep.

Put the chopped dates into a bowl, pour on the boiling water and stir in the baking soda. Set aside.

In a large bowl, beat the butter and sugar together until light and fluffy. Gradually add the beaten eggs, beating well after each addition.

Sift the flour and baking powder together over the mixture and fold in. Stir in the dates, along with their soaking water.

Spoon the mixture into the prepared pan and spread it evenly, right into the corners. Bake for 25–30 minutes, until firm and risen.

Meanwhile, to make the toffee sauce, heat the butter, sugar and cream together in a saucepan over a low heat until melted and smooth. Let it bubble for a few minutes until the sauce is thick enough to coat the back of a wooden spoon.

Heat your broiler to high. With a skewer, make holes all over the surface of the cooked sponge. Pour half of the toffee sauce over the sponge and put under the hot broiler for 2–3 minutes until the sauce is bubbling.

Cut the sponge into portions and serve with the remaining warm toffee sauce, and pouring cream or ice cream on the side.

Individual Lemon Sponges

Serves 6

Although they're not baked, these little steamed lemon sponges are so good that I had to include them. We have used steaming as one of the challenges on *The Great British Bake Off,* **as this age-old method really tests people's ability to know when something is cooked. It's a gentle technique, resulting in a very light and delicate dessert with an intense lemony flavor.**

—

6 tbsp lemon curd
(homemade or good-quality bought)

1 stick plus 2 tbsp (150g) butter, softened, plus extra to grease the molds

¾ cup (150g) superfine sugar

3 large eggs, beaten

Finely grated zest and juice of 1 lemon

1¼ cups (150g) all-purpose flour

2 tsp baking powder

Lightly grease six 6-oz (150ml) ramekins, or individual pudding molds, and line the base of each with a disc of parchment paper. Put 1 tablespoon lemon curd into the base of each mold.

In a large bowl, beat the butter and sugar together, using a hand-held electric whisk, until pale and creamy. Gradually incorporate the beaten eggs, beating well after each addition. Add the lemon zest and sift the flour and baking powder over the mixture. Using a spatula, fold to combine. Stir through the lemon juice.

Divide the mixture evenly between the ramekins. Cover each ramekin with a layer of parchment paper, then a layer of foil. Secure with string.

Stand the ramekins on a rack in a steamer or put them in a large saucepan and pour in enough boiling water to come halfway up their sides. Put the lid on and simmer gently for 40–50 minutes or until cooked through, topping up the water in the pan as necessary.

Carefully lift out the ramekins and remove the covers. Run a knife around the edge of each one to release the sponge and turn out onto warmed plates. Serve with crème anglaise or pouring cream.

Chocolate Soufflés

Serves 6–8

Made with bittersweet chocolate so they're not overly sweet, these individual soufflés are always an impressive way to end a meal. They're not as tricky as people think, holding their shape for at least three or four minutes when they come out of the oven. They are heavenly topped with a scoop of really good vanilla ice cream.

A little butter, to grease the ramekins

½ oz (15g) bittersweet chocolate, finely grated

1⅓ cups plus 1 tbsp (340g) whole milk

4 large eggs, separated

¾ cup plus 2 tbsp (180g) superfine sugar

5 tbsp (40g) unsweetened cocoa powder, plus extra to dust

2½ tbsp (30g) all-purpose flour

2 tbsp plus 1 tsp (25g) cornstarch

A pinch of fine salt

½ tsp lemon juice

———

Heat your oven to 400°F. Lightly butter 6–8 ramekins and coat the inside of each with grated chocolate (**1**). Put on a baking sheet.

Gently heat the milk in a saucepan until it is almost boiling. Meanwhile, in a bowl, mix the egg yolks with 6 tablespoons (70g) of the sugar to form a paste. Add the cocoa powder, flour and cornstarch and mix well.

Slowly pour the hot milk onto the egg mixture, whisking as you do so (**2**) and continue to whisk until fully combined. Return to the pan and cook over a low heat, stirring until the mixture is thickened and you have a smooth chocolate crème anglaise (**3**). Pour into a bowl, cover the surface closely with plastic wrap to prevent a skin forming and leave to cool slightly.

In a clean bowl, whisk the egg whites with the salt and lemon juice until stiff. Gradually whisk in the remaining ½ cup (110g) sugar, a spoonful at a time (**4**), to make a thick, glossy meringue.

Beat the chocolate crème anglaise until smooth and fold in a large spoonful of the meringue. Now add the remaining meringue mix and fold in gently (**5**) until evenly incorporated.

Divide the mixture between the prepared ramekins (**6**) and gently smooth the top to level. Run your thumb around the top of the ramekin to clean the edge and help the soufflé rise. Bake for 15–17 minutes until risen.

As you take the soufflés from the oven, dust them with a little sifted cocoa powder and serve straight away.

Steps illustrated overleaf

3

4

5

6

Baked Alaska

Serves 8

There's no denying that baking something which has ice cream in the middle is a test of the nerves. But it's actually very easy to do as long as you set your ice cream properly before you attempt to encase it with the meringue. This luscious strawberry and vanilla layered version is a total showstopper – well worth the effort.

_____

Sponge base

1 stick (125g butter), softened, plus extra to grease the pan

⅔ cup (125g) superfine sugar

2 large eggs

1 cup (125g) all-purpose flour

1½ tsp baking powder

Ice cream filling

2 cups (500g) strawberry ice cream

1¼ cups (300g) vanilla ice cream

Meringue

3 large egg whites

¼ tsp cream of tartar

¾ cup plus 2 tbsp (175g) superfine sugar

Heat your oven to 375°F. Grease the base of an 8-inch (20cm) springform pan and line with parchment paper.

In a large bowl, beat the butter and sugar together, using a hand-held electric whisk, until pale and fluffy. Beat in the eggs, one at a time, mixing well between each addition. Using a spatula, carefully fold the flour through the mixture until evenly combined.

Transfer the mixture to the prepared pan and gently smooth the surface. Bake for 20–25 minutes until the sponge is risen and springs back when it is lightly pressed in the center. Let the sponge cool in the pan for 5 minutes then remove and put on a wire rack to finish cooling.

Line a 6-cup (1.2L) bowl with plastic wrap. Beat the strawberry ice cream until soft then spread evenly over the base and around the side of the bowl to line it. Cover the ice cream layer with a sheet of plastic wrap and sit a smaller bowl in the center to create a hollow in the middle. Put in the freezer just long enough for the ice cream to set. Remove from the freezer and take out the smaller bowl. Fill the space with the vanilla ice cream then return to the freezer.

Heat your oven to 425°F. To make the meringue, whisk the egg whites to stiff peaks. Add the cream of tartar and a spoonful of sugar and whisk again. Continue to whisk in the sugar a spoonful at a time until you have a thick, glossy meringue.

Put the sponge in the middle of a baking sheet. Remove the ice cream bombe from the bowl, pulling on the plastic wrap to help release it. Turn the ice cream upside down and position centrally on the sponge. Remove the plastic wrap.

Spread the meringue over the bombe so it completely covers the ice cream and sponge base. Bake for 3–4 minutes until the meringue is just beginning to brown. Slide onto a serving plate and serve immediately.

White Chocolate and Raspberry Bread Pudding

Serves 4

Traditional bread pudding is a thing of joy. It's an old-fashioned recipe, so I've given it a modern update by adding white chocolate and fresh raspberries. Don't be afraid to leave it in the oven for a few minutes longer so it takes on a bit of dark color, as that's where the flavor comes in.

5 tbsp (75g) butter, plus extra to grease the dish

8 slices white bread, crusts removed

1 cup (125g) raspberries

½ cup (100g) white chocolate chips

Scant 1 cup (225g) whole milk

Scant 1 cup (225g) heavy cream

1 vanilla bean, split and seeds scraped out

3 large eggs

2 tbsp (25g) superfine sugar

To finish

3 tbsp apricot preserves

¼ cup (25g) confectioners' sugar

———

Heat your oven to 350°F. Grease a 4-cup (1L) baking dish.

Butter the slices of bread. Cover the base of the baking dish with a layer of buttered bread. Scatter over half of the raspberries and half of the white chocolate chips.

Layer the remaining bread slices on top and scatter over the remaining raspberries and chocolate chips.

In a saucepan over a medium-low heat, heat the milk and cream together with the vanilla seeds. Beat the eggs and sugar together in a bowl, then pour on the hot creamy milk, stirring as you do so. Carefully pour the egg mix over the bread.

Stand the baking dish in a deep roasting pan and pour enough cold water into the pan to come about 1 inch (2½cm) up the side of the dish. Bake for 30 minutes or until the pudding is just set and golden.

In a small saucepan, heat the apricot preserves with a splash of water, then pass through a strainer; set aside.

Dust the pudding with confectioners' sugar and wave a kitchen torch over the surface to caramelize . Brush with the warm apricot glaze and serve, with Devonshire clotted cream or ice cream if you like.

Banoffee Pie

Serves 6–8

Banoffee pie is a popular British dessert and the name comes from the combination of the caramel toffee and banana filling. If you have a sweet tooth, this is the dessert for you! Instead of a pie crust, which can often go a bit soggy, I've used a crunchy walnut and cracker crumb. It contrasts beautifully with the sweet and creamy caramel and banana filling.

Base

6 oz (about 12 sheets/175g) graham crackers

¾ cup (75g) walnuts

1 stick plus 1 tbsp (125g) butter, melted

Caramel banana filling

1 stick plus 1 tbsp (125g) butter

⅔ cup (125g) dark brown sugar

1 x 13.4-oz (380g) can dulce de leche (or 1⅓ cups of other caramel)

A pinch of sea salt

4–5 ripe bananas

Topping

1¼ cups (300g) heavy cream

⅔ cup (60g) walnut pieces

1 tbsp unsweetened cocoa powder

To make the base, using a blender or food processor, blitz the graham crackers and walnuts together to a crumb-like texture. Tip into a bowl and stir in the melted butter to coat the crumbs fully.

Tip the crumb mixture into a 9-inch (23cm) tart pan with removable base, 1½ inches (4cm) deep, spread evenly and press down firmly onto the base. Put on a baking sheet.

For the filling, in a heavy-based saucepan over a medium-low heat, melt the butter with the sugar until the sugar is dissolved. Add the dulce de leche with the salt and bring to a boil, stirring. Boil steadily for 5–6 minutes until large bubbles appear on the surface and the mixture thickens slightly to make a smooth caramel sauce. Leave to cool for 5 minutes.

Roughly chop the bananas and stir them through the caramel sauce. Pour the mixture over the nutty crumb base and spread out evenly. Put in the fridge to set for 30 minutes.

When ready to serve, whip the cream to soft peaks and spread over the set caramel base. Scatter over the walnut pieces and dust with cocoa powder.

Lime Meringue Pie

Serves 6–8

My mother used to make an amazing lemon meringue pie and this is my twist on her classic recipe, using lime instead which I think gives it more of a kick. The textures are incredible – a crispy base, a beautiful tartness from the creamy filling and the light billowing cloud of sweet meringue on top.

———

Pastry

1⅔ cups (200g) all-purpose flour, plus extra to dust

7 tbsp (100g) cold butter, diced

1 large egg, beaten

About 2 tbsp cold water

1 egg yolk, beaten with 1 tsp milk, to seal the pie crust

Filling

1⅔ cups (400g) water

Finely grated zest and juice of 4 limes

½ cup (45g) cornstarch, mixed to a slurry with 3 tbsp cold water

¾ cup (150g) superfine sugar

3 large egg yolks

3 tbsp (50g) unsalted butter, in pieces

Meringue

3 large egg whites

¾ cup (150g) superfine sugar

To make the pastry, put the flour into a large bowl and add the butter. Using your fingers, rub the butter into the flour until it resembles fine breadcrumbs. Mix in the beaten egg, using a dinner knife, then mix in the water 1 tablespoon at a time until the mixture starts to come together and form a ball. Turn out onto a lightly floured work surface and knead briefly until smooth. Wrap in parchment paper or plastic wrap and chill for at least 30 minutes before baking.

On a lightly floured surface, roll out the pastry thinly and use to line a lightly greased 9-inch (23cm) tart pan with removable base, 1½ inches (4cm) deep. Prick the base with a fork and chill for 20 minutes.

Heat your oven to 400°F. Put the tart pan on a baking sheet. Line the pie crust with parchment paper, add a layer of baking beans and bake 'blind' for 15 minutes. Remove the paper and beans and return the pie crust to the oven for 5 minutes to dry the base. Now brush the inside of the pie crust with the egg yolk mix and return to the oven for 2 minutes to seal the base. Remove the pie crust and lower the oven temperature to 325°F.

For the filling, in a saucepan over a medium heat, bring the water to a boil with the lime zest and juice added. Stir in the cornstarch slurry and cook, stirring, for 1–2 minutes until thickened. Add the sugar and stir until dissolved. Remove from the heat and let cool slightly, then beat in the egg yolks. Return the pan to a low heat and cook for 2–3 minutes. Add the butter and stir until melted. Pour the filling into the pie crust and leave to cool completely.

For the meringue, in a large, clean bowl, whisk the egg whites until stiff peaks form. Gradually whisk in the sugar, a spoonful at a time, until it is all incorporated and you have a stiff, glossy meringue.

Spoon the meringue over the lime filling, spreading it out to give a good seal with the edge of the pie crust. Swirl the surface decoratively with an offset spatula knife. Bake for 40 minutes until the meringue is crisp and golden. Carefully remove the pie from the pan and leave to cool slightly before serving.

Mango and Passion Fruit Trifle

Serves 8

Trifle has been around in the UK since at least the eighteenth century and was particularly popular as a seventies dinner party dessert. My version of this classic has a white chocolate crème anglaise filling and a mascarpone and cream topping, offset by fresh fruit and a mango gelatin. Perhaps it's a bit of a stretch to include it in this book, but it's one of my all-time favorites!

1¼ tsp unflavored gelatin powder

1⅔ cups (400g) mango juice

12–16 savoiardi cookies

1 ripe mango

2 passion fruit

Crème anglaise

⅔ cup (150g) whole milk

⅔ cup (150g) heavy cream

1 tsp vanilla extract

4 large egg yolks

⅓ cup (80g) superfine sugar

1 tbsp cornstarch

4 oz (100g) white chocolate, chopped

Topping

1 cup (250g) mascarpone

1 cup (250g) heavy cream

2 passion fruit, halved

———

Put 2 tablespoons of water in a medium-sized heatproof bowl, sprinkle the gelatin over and set aside to hydrate.

Heat the mango juice in a small saucepan over a low heat; do not boil. Remove from the heat. Add ¼ cup of the warm mango juice to the gelatin and stir until the gelatin has fully dissolved. Add the gelatin to the mango juice in the saucepan and mix until well combined, then let cool slightly.

Cover the base of a 2-quart (2-liter) trifle bowl with the savoiardi cookies, breaking them up to fit. Peel the mango and slice the flesh away from the pit. Arrange the mango slices over the savoiardi cookies. Halve the passion fruit, scoop out the pulp with a teaspoon and dot over the mango layer. Pour the liquid mango mixture over to cover. Chill for 2 hours until set.

To make the crème anglaise, in a saucepan over a medium-low heat, heat the milk and cream together until it just begins to boil. Remove from the heat. Whisk the egg yolks, sugar and cornstarch together in a bowl, then pour on the hot creamy milk, stirring as you do so.

Return the mixture to the pan, add the white chocolate and stir over a low heat until the chocolate is melted and the crème anglaise is smooth and well thickened. Pass through a strainer into a pitcher and cover the surface closely with plastic wrap to prevent a skin forming. Leave to cool for 10 minutes.

Pour the crème anglaise over the set gelatin and chill for another 2 hours.

To finish, whip the mascarpone with the cream until holding soft peaks, then spoon over the crème anglaise. Decorate with the passion fruit pulp and serve.

Berry Pavlova

Serves 8

Desserts can sometimes feel a bit wintry, but this berry pavlova is perfect for summer dining. Mounds of juicy fresh berries sitting on gently whipped cream and scattered with fresh mint leaves, all resting on a perfectly crisp and chewy meringue – it's a real taste of hot, sunny days.

4 large egg whites

1 cup plus 2 tbsp (225g) superfine sugar

1 tsp white wine vinegar

1 tsp cornstarch

Topping

1½ cups (350g) heavy cream

1 cup (150g) halved or quartered strawberries

1¼ cups (150g) raspberries

1½ cups (150g) redcurrants

1 cup (100g) blueberries

To finish

Finely grated zest of 1 lemon

Few sprigs of mint

Heat your oven to 350°F. Line a large large baking sheet with a sheet of parchment paper.

In a large, clean bowl, whisk the egg whites until they form stiff peaks. Gradually whisk in the superfine sugar, a spoonful at a time, until it is all incorporated and you have a thick, glossy meringue. Fold in the wine vinegar and cornstarch.

Spread the meringue into a circle, about 9 inches (23cm) in diameter, on the lined baking sheet. Bake for 1 hour, then switch off the oven and leave the pavlova inside to cool completely.

Whip the cream in a bowl to soft peaks then spread over the top of the cooled meringue. Arrange the berry fruits on top, grate over a little lemon zest and finish with a scattering of mint leaves.

Mango Meringue Roulade

Serves 8

A meringue roulade always makes a stunning centerpiece dessert. This lighter version is filled with mango cream and fresh mango pieces, while coconut chips add extra texture. The only step that needs careful attention is rolling the meringue around the mango filling. Go steadily and firmly, using the parchment paper to support the meringue as you roll.

4 large egg whites
1¼ cups (250g) superfine sugar
2 tbsp coconut chips

Filling
1 mango
Scant 1 cup (200g) heavy cream
⅔ cup (150g) thick Greek yogurt
7 tbsp (100g) canned mango pulp

To finish
Confectioners' sugar, to dust

—

Heat your oven to 400°F. Grease and line a jelly roll pan about 13 x 9 inches (32 x 22cm) with parchment paper.

In a large, clean bowl, whisk the egg whites until they form stiff peaks (**1**). Gradually whisk in the sugar, a spoonful at a time, until it is all incorporated and you have a thick, glossy meringue.

Spread the mixture evenly in the prepared pan (**2**) and scatter over the coconut chips. Bake for 15–20 minutes until risen, lightly golden and set.

Have a large sheet of parchment paper ready. Carefully invert the meringue onto the paper (**3**). Peel away the lining paper (**4**) and leave to cool.

Meanwhile, prepare the filling. Peel the mango, cut the flesh from the pit, then cut into ¼-inch (5mm) dice. In a large bowl, whip the cream until it holds soft peaks. Fold in the yogurt and swirl through the mango pulp. Spread the mango cream evenly over the meringue (**5**) and scatter over the diced mango.

Lightly score an indentation along the meringue, about 1 inch (2½cm) in from the edge of one of the long sides. Now, using the paper to help you, start to roll from this edge to form an even roulade (**6**). Chill for 30 minutes before serving.

Dust the roulade lightly with confectioners' sugar before serving (**7**).

Steps illustrated overleaf

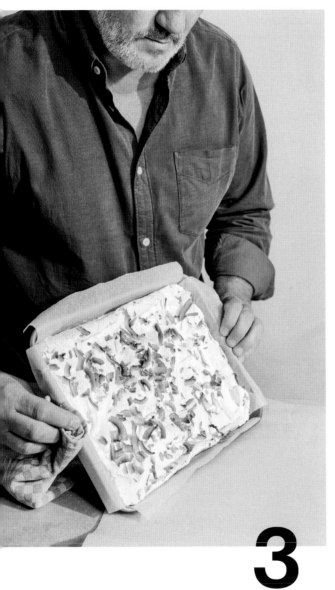

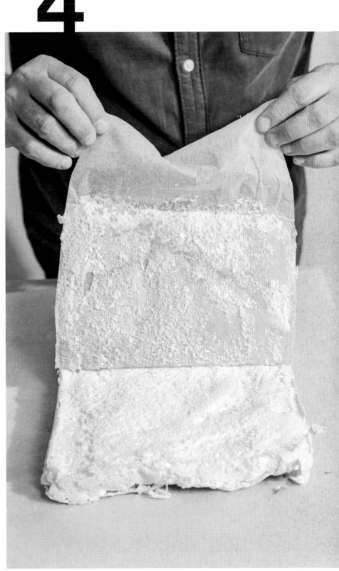

5

6

Lemon Tartlets

Makes 5

Crisp buttery pastry is filled with a silky smooth, intensely lemony filling in these elegant tartlets. Piping in the filling gives a neater finish and the pearl sugar sprinkled over the top provides a little extra crunch to complete my take on this timeless dessert.

Pastry

1¼ cups (150g) all-purpose flour

2 tbsp confectioners' sugar

1 stick (110g) cold unsalted **butter**, diced, plus extra to grease the pans

1 egg yolk

½ tsp lemon juice

1 tbsp cold water

Filling

6 large eggs

1½ tbsp cornstarch

Finely grated zest and juice of 4 lemons

¾ cup plus 1 tbsp (165g) superfine sugar

1 stick plus 2 tbsp (150g) unsalted butter, diced

To finish

Pearl sugar

———

To make the pastry, mix the flour and confectioners' sugar together in a large bowl and add the butter. Using your fingers, rub the butter into the flour mixture until the mixture resembles fine breadcrumbs. Make a well in the center and add the egg yolk, lemon juice and water. Mix, using a dinner knife, until the pastry comes together; if it's a little dry add a splash more water.

Knead the pastry gently to form a smooth ball then wrap in parchment paper or plastic wrap and chill for at least 30 minutes.

Heat your oven to 400°F. Lightly grease 5 individual tart pans, about 4 inches (10cm) in diameter.

On a lightly floured surface, roll out the pastry to a ⅛-inch (3mm) thickness and use to line the tart pans, leaving the excess overhanging the edge of the pans. Prick the bases with a fork.

Line the tartlet crusts with parchment paper and add a layer of baking beans. Bake 'blind' for 8 minutes then remove the paper and beans and return to the oven for 5 minutes until the pastry looks dry and is pale in color. Use a small, sharp knife to trim away the excess pastry from the edge. Leave to cool.

To make the filling, in a large bowl, whisk the eggs with the cornstarch until smoothly combined. Put the lemon zest and juice into a saucepan with the sugar and bring to a boil. Pour a little of this mixture onto the whisked eggs, whisking as you do so, then pour the egg mixture into the pan and return to the heat. Simmer for 1 minute, whisking all the time.

Remove from the heat then add the butter, a little at the time, whisking after each addition. Pour the lemon filling into a bowl, cover the surface closely with plastic wrap to prevent a skin forming, and leave to cool.

Once cooled, put the lemon filling into a pastry bag fitted with a ½-inch (1cm) plain tip, and pipe into the prepared tartlet crusts, in a spiral from the edge towards the center. Sprinkle with pearl sugar to finish.

Yule Log

Serves 10

A chocolate yule log is always a welcome festive treat but adding a touch of orange liqueur takes this one to another level, and the whipped cream filling balances the rich chocolate buttercream frosting perfectly.

———

A little vegetable oil, to grease the pan

6 oz (150g) semisweet chocolate (45% cocoa solids), broken into small pieces

6 large eggs, separated

¾ cup (150g) superfine sugar, plus extra to sprinkle

2 tbsp unsweetened cocoa powder, sifted

Filling

1⅔ cups (400g) heavy cream

A splash of orange liqueur, such as Grand Marnier or Cointreau

Chocolate buttercream

2 sticks plus 3 tbsp (270g) butter, at room temperature

4 cups (400g) confectioners' sugar

9½ oz (270g) semisweet chocolate (45% cocoa solids), melted

To finish

Confectioners' sugar, to dust
Orange-flavored chocolate, for grating

Heat your oven to 400°F. Line the base and sides of a 11 x 16-inch (27 x 39cm) jelly roll pan with parchment paper and brush the paper with oil.

Melt the chocolate in a heatproof bowl over a saucepan of simmering water, making sure the base of the bowl is not touching the water. Leave to cool slightly.

Using an electric hand whisk, beat the egg yolks and sugar together in a bowl until thick and creamy. Carefully fold the cooled chocolate into the egg mixture. Add the cocoa powder and fold in until smoothly combined.

In a separate, clean bowl, whisk the egg whites until stiff. Gently stir a large spoonful into the chocolate mixture to lighten it, then carefully fold in the rest of the whisked egg whites. Pour the mixture into the prepared pan and bake for 18–20 minutes, until the sponge is risen and just firm to touch.

Turn out the cooked sponge onto a sheet of parchment paper dusted with superfine sugar and carefully remove the lining paper. Cover the sponge with a clean, damp kitchen towel and leave to cool completely.

To make the buttercream, melt the chocolate (as above) and let cool slightly. Beat the butter and confectioners' sugar together in a bowl until smooth, add the cooled melted chocolate and mix well to combine.

About an hour before serving, remove the towel from the cooled sponge and drizzle a splash of orange liqueur evenly over the surface. Whip the cream to soft peaks then spread evenly over the sponge, almost to the edges.

Roll up the sponge from the long side towards you, using the paper to help. Cut a slice off at an angle from one end. Put the roll on a serving plate and attach the slice so that it looks like a branch. Using an offset spatula, spread the buttercream over the chocolate log, leaving the ends uncovered. Use a fork to mark lines and create a bark effect. Put in the fridge until ready to serve.

Just before serving, dust the chocolate log with confectioners' sugar and sprinkle with grated orange-flavored chocolate.

Classic Meringues

Makes 7

Meringues are a versatile bake and I think it's a great skill to learn how to make them properly. The perfect meringue should be light, crispy on the outside but still a little gooey and chewy inside. You achieve this by cooking them at a low heat for a fairly long time and letting them cool off in the still-warm oven. You can serve them simply with whipped cream, as I have done here, or turn them into a dessert called Eton Mess: break the meringues into pieces and fold through lightly whipped cream with a mix of puréed and chopped strawberries.

6 large egg whites

1⅓ cups plus 1 tbsp (280g) superfine sugar

2 tsp cornstarch

1 cup (250g) heavy cream, whipped, to serve

———

Heat your oven to 275°F (if you have a convection oven do not use the convection setting). Line a large baking sheet with parchment paper.

Using a hand-held electric whisk or stand mixer, whisk the egg whites in a large, clean bowl on a low speed for 1 minute. Increase the speed to medium and continue to whisk until the egg white stands in stiff peaks when the beaters are lifted. Do not over-whisk.

Now turn the speed up to high and start adding the sugar, a tablespoonful at a time, at 30-second intervals. Once all the sugar is added, scrape down the sides of the bowl and continue to whisk until the meringue is thick and glossy. Be careful not to over-mix, as your meringue will go grainy. Sift the cornstarch over the surface and fold in gently.

Using a large metal spoon, scoop up mounds of meringue and put on the prepared baking sheet, leaving plenty of space in between them.

Bake in the oven for 1 hour, then turn the oven off and open the door. Leave the meringues to cool inside with the door slightly ajar for 3 hours or until the oven is completely cold.

Serve the meringues with whipped cream.

Chocolate and Raspberry Entremets

Serves 10–12

Boasting a fantastic combination of flavors, this is the most challenging recipe in the book and an absolute showstopper. You'll feel a real sense of accomplishment when you serve it to your very impressed guests! There are several elements to complete, but each one is actually not that difficult. Just take it slowly and you'll be fine. For the best finish, freeze the entremets overnight and allow 3–4 hours to thaw before serving. The preserves should also be made at least 2 hours in advance to give them enough time to freeze solid. Alternatively, you can use 1 cup (250g) store-bought good-quality jam.

Raspberry preserves
⅓ cup (70g) superfine sugar
½ tsp pectin powder
Juice of ½ lemon
1⅔ cups (175g) raspberries

Chocolate Genoise sponge
4 large eggs
⅔ cup (125g) superfine sugar
1 tsp vanilla extract
¾ cup (100g) all-purpose flour
⅓ cup (30g) unsweetened cocoa powder
2 tbsp (25g) butter, melted and cooled

Ingredients continued overleaf

For the raspberry preserves layer
Heat the sugar, pectin powder and lemon juice in a saucepan over a medium heat to dissolve the sugar. Bring to a simmer, add the raspberries and let simmer for 10–12 minutes, until they break down and the mixture starts to thicken. Line an 8-inch (20cm) springform pan (or a similar-sized small baking sheet) with plastic wrap. Pour in the raspberry jam, leave to cool then freeze for a minimum of 1 hour.

To make the Genoise sponge
Heat your oven to 400°F and line an 8-inch (20cm) springform pan with parchment paper. Using a stand mixer fitted with the whisk attachment, whisk the eggs, sugar and vanilla extract together for 8–10 minutes until the mixture is pale in color and tripled in volume. Sift the flour and cocoa powder together into a separate bowl. Using a spatula, carefully fold half of the flour mix into the whisked mixture; make sure you don't knock out the air. Fold in the rest of the flour mix, then slowly pour in the melted butter, gently folding it in as you pour.

Pour the mixture into the prepared pan and bake for 15–18 minutes until the cake is risen and just starting to shrink from the side of the pan. To check it is cooked, insert a skewer into the center; if it comes out clean the cake is ready. Leave in the pan for a few minutes, then remove to a wire rack to finish cooling.

Once cooled, ensure that the sponge is level; if it has a hump on top slice it off with a serrated knife. Also, the sponge needs to be slightly smaller than the pan so, using a serrated knife, carefully trim off about ¼ inch (5mm) all around the outside. You should now have a sponge about 7¾ inches (19cm) in diameter. Set aside.

Continued overleaf

Chocolate and raspberry crisp

4 oz (100g) good-quality milk chocolate, broken into pieces

1 cup (30g) puffed rice

¼ cup (10g) freeze-dried raspberries

Chocolate mousse

6 oz (150g) bittersweet chocolate, broken into pieces

¾ tsp unflavored gelatin powder

½ cup (125g) whole milk

1 tsp vanilla bean paste or vanilla extract

1 cup plus 2 tbsp (270g) heavy cream

¼ cup (50g) superfine sugar

Ingredients continued overleaf

For the chocolate and raspberry crisp layer

Line the base of an 8-inch (20cm) springform pan with parchment paper and the side with a 2½-inch (6cm) deep length of clear acetate or oiled parchment paper.

Melt the chocolate in a heatproof bowl over a saucepan of simmering water, then mix in the puffed rice and dried raspberries. Press the mixture onto the base of the springform pan, using the back of a metal spoon or offset spatula, making sure it is flat and there are no gaps. Chill for at least 30 minutes to set.

Chocolate mousse

Just before assembling the entremets, melt the chocolate in a heatproof bowl over a saucepan of simmering water, making sure that the bowl is not touching the water. Meanwhile, put 1½ tablespoons of water in a medium-sized heatproof bowl, sprinkle over the gelatin and set aside to hydrate. In a small pan, bring the milk to a boil with the vanilla added. Take off the heat.

Add ¼ cup (60g) of the hot milk to the gelatin and stir until fully dissolved, then pour the gelatin mixture into the remaining milk and stir until well combined. Slowly pour this milk into the melted chocolate, stirring as you do so. It may start to look split or thicken quickly but keep stirring and it will become smooth and shiny.

Using a hand-held electric whisk, whisk the cream with the sugar until soft peaks form. Carefully fold into the chocolate mixture until fully incorporated.

To assemble the entremets

Remove the springform pan containing the chocolate crisp from the fridge. Pour about one-quarter of the chocolate mousse onto the chocolate crisp and level with an offset spatula or the back of a metal spoon.

Slice the Genoise sponge horizontally in half, to give two even layers. Carefully position one of the sponge layers on the mousse, leaving a small margin around the edge. Cover with another one-quarter of the chocolate mousse.

Now take the preserves from the freezer and remove from the pan. Working quickly, cut a 7½-inch (19cm) circle. Peel off the plastic wrap and put the preserves on top the sponge layer in the pan. Pour half of the remaining chocolate mousse on top of the preserves to cover it completely and fill the gap around the edge.

Continued overleaf

Raspberry glaze

1 cup (100g) raspberries
(frozen or fresh)

**½ tsp unflavored gelatin
powder**

¼ cup (50g) superfine sugar

1 tbsp just-boiled water

To decorate

Fresh raspberries

Herbs or edible flowers

Position the other sponge layer centrally on top, again leaving a small gap around the edge. Pour the remaining chocolate mousse on top, making sure it fills the gap too. Level with a small offset spatula or the back of a metal spoon. Chill in the fridge for 30 minutes. (In the meantime, make the glaze.)

To make the raspberry glaze

Using a blender, blitz the raspberries to a purée then pass through a fine strainer into a small saucepan. Put 1 tablespoon of water in a medium-sized heatproof bowl, sprinkle over the gelatin and set aside to hydrate. Add the sugar to the raspberry purée and bring to a boil then take off the heat. Pour the 1 tablespoon of just-boiled water onto the gelatin and stir until fully dissolved, then stir the gelatin into the hot raspberry mixture until well combined. Leave to cool for 20–30 minutes.

Once cooled, pour the raspberry glaze on top of the entremets. Gently shake the pan from side to side to make sure the glaze is even. Carefully put the entremets in the freezer, ensuring the pan is level. Leave to freeze overnight.

To prepare the dessert for serving

About 3–4 hours ahead, take the dessert out of the freezer. Remove from the pan and peel off the acetate while still frozen. Leave to thaw in the fridge for 3–4 hours.

Just before serving, decorate the entremets with raspberries and herbs (I like to use small mint or basil leaves) or edible flowers.

Index

Acknowledgments

I'm dedicating this book to my Mum, Jill, and my Dad, John, for getting me into baking at an early stage and giving me my career... and, obviously, for being my Mum and Dad!

Massive thanks to my agents, Geraldine, Anna and Kate, for their patience and hard work.

From Bloomsbury, I'd like to thank the team who have helped with this book: Rowan Yapp, Lena Hall, Joel Arcanjo, Laura Brodie, Philippa Cotton, Akua Boateng and Don Shanahan.

To Claire Bassano (legend), Laura Bayliss, Janet Illsley, Liz Haarala and Max Hamilton, Nikki Dupin, Lola Brandelli, Jen Kay and Caroline Stearns, I couldn't have done the book without you; you're all amazing, thank you!

BLOOMSBURY PUBLISHING
Bloomsbury Publishing Plc
1385 Broadway, New York, NY 10018, USA

BLOOMSBURY, BLOOMSBURY PUBLISHING, and the Diana logo
are trademarks of Bloomsbury Publishing Plc

First published in Great Britain 2022
First published in the United States of America 2022

Library of Congress Cataloging-in-Publication Data is available.

ISBN: HB: 978-1-63557-929-1
eBook: 978-1-63557-930-7
signed edition: 978-1-63973-124-4

10 9 8 7 6 5 4 3 2 1

Project editor: Janet Illsley
Art Direction & Design: Nikki Dupin at Studio Nic & Lou
Photography: Liz & Max Haarala Hamilton
Food Styling: Claire Bassano
Prop Styling: Jennifer Kay
Americanization: Caroline Stearns

Printed in Germany by Mohn Media

To find out more about our authors and books visit www.bloomsbury.com
and sign up for our newsletters.

Bloomsbury books may be purchased for business or promotional use.
For information on bulk purchases please contact Macmillan Corporate and
Premium Sales Department at specialmarkets@macmillan .com.